)

the black kalendar of coventry

twelve true stories of murder and mayhem

adam wood

MANGO

Published by

Mango Books
18 Soho Square
London
W1D 3QL

ISBN: 978-1-914277-41-2

www.AdamWoodHistory.com

the black kalendar of coventry

twelve true stories of murder and mayhem

adam wood

MANGO

Published by

Mango Books
18 Soho Square
London
W1D 3QL

ISBN: 978-1-914277-41-2

www.AdamWoodHistory.com

the black kalendar of coventry

twelve true stories
of murder and mayhem

For Bruce Collie,
whose treasured
*Black Kalendar
of Aberdeen*
was the inspiration
for this volume.

INTRODUCTION

A book is never written by just one person, even if they're the one who has spent hours at the computer researching a long-forgotten case involving people perhaps not even their own descendants know anything about. No; someone will spark an idea through an innocent comment, or impart some nugget of informaton which, although not apparently important at face value, can provide the link between one person and another.

When my book *The Watchmaker's Revenge* was published in October last year Paul Sheehan gave a very kind review, innocently asking what the next Coventry-based true crime book would be... "There had to be loads of murders in the old days," he said. So I went away and spent a couple of days trawling the British Newspaper Archive website, even with a cursory glance uncovering at least forty such cases from the Victorian era. Although Paul didn't know it, he provided the spark which resulted in my collecting dozens of dark deeds in Coventry, from drunken antics to cold-blooded murder.

But how to present them? My friend Bruce Collie had for some time quite rightly crowed about his prized volume *The Black Kalendar of Aberdeen*, and this gave me the idea of presenting the Coventry cases in a similar chronological format. Doing so we're able to see promotions for Coventry City policemen as the years pass, and note the same judges, coroners and solicitors appearing in that passage of time.

The first *Black Kalendar of Coventry* presents a twelve cases datings from 1820 to 1874. Further volumes are in preparation, and will provide a window into the dark underbelly of Coventry in the Victorian era.

Adam Wood
Chapelfields, November 2022

ells said if he was my prisoner he quietly, but he did not want to be en took him to the Station House. to the Station House I told Sergeant e against Wells, and he at once sent Dawson to come and sign it. I went son at the house in Bradford street. h me, and on the road to the Station whether he should charge Wells with stinely removing. After going back use it was time for me to go on my t therefore say what else passed.

High street, and Thomas Holding, gave ence.

the case for the prosecution.

n spoke for the defence, and contended red no obstruction to Mr. Wells re- and that Wells would insist upon ustody.

ed Mr. O'Brien whether he seriously them believe that plaintiff was so in tion House as to insist upon being er or not?

uch are my instructions, my Lord.

o said—I am a furniture broker, and reet, Coventry. The house No. 19, is my property. On the 15th of rson named Moore occupied the house, quarters' rent. I went down to the ing of that day, and saw Wells and ng down a loom. I told Wells I was use, and he must not touch the loom. ld, for it belonged to him. I then n from the Station House. I certainly ells I would have him locked up when ls was in a very excited state, and ten sword over his head. He was so d of him. I afterwards went to the h Police Constable Russell, but did gainst Wells. I said I would sign a for clandestinely removing a part of ns said he could not take that charge. ould not leave the Station House, and rn him out, neck and crop.

by Mr. Macaulay—When I took the to the house I told him to let Wells the right or the left, see where it take him into custody. I remember let down out of the window, and I ack into the house again.

e Kemp deposed—I was fetched by adford street, Hill-fields, on the 15th to prevent a breach of the peace. I l several others there. Mr. Wells was There was no obstruction offered to have taken the loom away if he had instructions to take him into custody, event a breach of the peace, and see loom to. Wells was in a very excited me several times to take him into ered me so that at last I ran into an of his way. I then sent for Police to assist me in preventing a breach of watch where the loom was taken to. ere not to take Wells in custody. I he had done so until he came back for charge.

by Mr. Macaulay—I believe a part of ut of the window, and when it got to hen took it back again into the house. the men were. I believe it was Mr. of his men.

Salmons deposed—On the 15th of ssell brought Mr. Wells to the Station ge of stealing part of a loom from a street, belonging to Mr. Dawson. I r Mr. Dawson to come and sign the wson came he said he should not charge but clandestinely removing a part of n I could not take such a charge. I turn Wells out of the Station House. present to give bail for him, and when ge signed against him I told him he ed to lock the door.

itnesses were called, but they merely vidence of Mr. Dawson as to his not ustody.

aid it was not necessary to call any

replied, and said, the evidence of s sufficient proof that plaintiff had stody, because Dawson was willing to st him, although not for stealing.

en summed up. He said defendant ause any good by bringing up things 14 or 16 years before, in order to ter of plaintiff. Even if it was true, f e k that ought now to have been r did he like the manner in which the defence gave their evidence. They all ating a taught lesson. It had been plaintiff was given in charge and tion House by a Policeman and a

clined his addresses. It was also stated that the prisoner's father and mother had died suddenly, and had exhibited symptoms of insanity. It was further shown that on the day the child was drowned the prisoner had appeared in a melancholy and desponding state of mind.

Mr Leigh replied on behalf of the Crown, and his Lordship summed up at great length, pointing out the law relative to the case, but cautioning the Jury against what was sometimes urged, that the enormity of a crime was presumptive evidence of insanity.

The Jury, with little hesitation, returned a verdict of "*Not Guilty*, on the ground of insanity."

STEALING FOWLS AT FOLESHILL.—*John Phillips*, 35 weaver, was indicted for having, at Foleshill, on the 16th of July last, stolen two fowls, some eggs, and candles, the property of William Rowley.

Mr. Adams prosecuted.

The evidence showed that the prisoner had been at the prosecutor's house on the night in question, but it was not clear that he committed the robbery, and the Jury *Acquitted* the prisoner.

ACT OF AN IDIOT.—*Sarah Schinar* was charged with having, at Foleshill, on the 23rd of July last, maliciously thrown some boiling water over Sussannah Smart, with intent to do her bodily harm.

It was proved by the evidence of Mr. Blenkinsop, surgeon, that the prisoner was an idiot, and the Learned Judge directed the Jury to return a verdict of *Not Guilty*. He also ordered the prisoner to be taken care of by the authorities.

CHARGE OF MURDER AT COVENTRY.

Frederick King, 48, weaver, was charged with having, at Coventry, on the 5th of May last, wilfully murdered his wife, Eliza King. He was also charged on a Coroner's Inquisition with the manslaughter of the said Eliza King.

Mr. Adams appeared for the prosecution.

The evidence was exactly the same as that given before the Coroner's Jury and the Magistrates, and published in the *Coventry Herald* at the time of the commitment of prisoner.

After the evidence for the prosecution had been gone through, the prisoner then read a statement to the effect that on Sunday, the 5th of May, he missed two pairs of trousers and a pair of boots. He asked deceased about them, and she said she had stolen them. He then told her that she was a bad woman, and that it was no wonder that their son Frederick should rob his master when she set him such a bad example. She was not in want of anything. He brought some mackarel home for dinner, she had had three 4lb. loaves, and he gave her a shilling, and left the money for the rent, so that she had no occasion to make away with his things. Prisoner alluded generally to what he said was bad conduct on his wife's part; but he wished to God she had got better. He solemnly declared that he never raised his hands against deceased, and did no more than push

It appeared from the evidence that the plaintiff is the proprietor of the Borough Bank, Wolverhampton, and also a metal broker in a large way of business in South Staffordshire, the defendant being a lawyer and banker, residing at Wolverhampton. In 1861 plaintiff entered into a composition with a majority of his creditors, and they left the whole of his business in his hands as before. Defendant, Mr. Duignan, represented a Mr. Bayley, a creditor of plaintiff's, and one who did not enter into the composition. Mr. Bayley seemed determined to get his money from plaintiff if possible, and therefore had taken proceedings against Mr. Griffiths for the recovery of his money, and according to the new law, when a man entered an action he might get a discovery from the defendant by administering questions, which the defendant was bound to answer upon oath. If he did not answer them he was liable to a process attachment, upon which he might be taken into custody by the Sheriff. An attachment is a writ issued from one of the superior Courts, and is a common means adopted for enforcing the payment of money, whether due under a rule of Court or a Judge's order. An attachment may also be issued for any contempt of Court, and is also issued for neglect to answer interrogatories which may be put. On the 4th of July last Mr. Duignan, on behalf of his client Mr. Bayley, had put a number of interrogatories to Mr. Griffiths, which he had refused to answer, in consequence of which an attachment was issued against Mr. Griffiths, and a Sheriff's officer was sent to execute it, but in consequence of Mr. Griffiths keeping his door locked the attachment was not executed. On that day Mr. Duignan was at the Quarter Sessions at Walsall, and left a note with Mr. Barnes, the Walsall reporter and correspondent of the *Birmingham Journal* and *Daily Post*, to the effect that Mr. Griffiths was in custody of the Sheriff under an attachment issued against him in an action at the suit of James Bayley. On the strength of this note Mr. Barnes sent a paragraph to the *Journal* and *Post*, which appeared next day, and which constituted the libel complained of.

her away from him to avoid her violence. He called his son, Henry King, a child about nine years of age.

The prisoner—Did you see me strike your mother?

Witness—You struck her once.

DEBT.—Clark *v.* Poole.—Mr. Kennedy, instructe Mr. East, was Counsel for the plaintiff, and Mr. Ser O'Brien, instructed by Mr. Stokes, of Dudley, fo defendant.

The plaintiff, James Clark, is a blacksmith at Bromwich, and the defendant is a carrier and dealer at Great Bridge. The action was broug recover £5. 1s., the balance of an account for delivered, and for £20 for certain goods entrusted t defendant as carrier to deliver, but which were delivered. The plaintiff's case was that he had sol defendant a quantity of scrap iron, on which th fendant owed £5. 1s.; and that on the occasion o removal, some two years ago, he employed the de ant to remove his tools to his new house. The de ant, he said, took them from the one house, but di take them to the other. He gave no reason fo proceeding.

The defence was that the balance was not due that the goods were handed over to the defenda sell when the plaintiff was "in difficulties;" that h so sell them for £2; and that he kept the money account" of something the plaintiff owed him.

The Jury gave a verdict for the plaintiff—dam one farthing.

DISPUTE CONCERNING A MACHINE.—Field *v.* Glas —Mr. Sergeant Hayes and Mr. Field, instructed by Taynton, were Counsel for the plaintiff; and Macaulay, Q.C., with Mr. Wills, instructed by Jagger, were Counsel for the defendant.

The plaintiff, Richard Finch Field, is a baker, in St. Swithin's-street, Worcester, and the defend David Glasgow, is a machinist, carrying on busine Birmingham. The declaration alleged that the de ant had promised to manufacture and deliver with reasonable period a certain machine; that plaintiff paid £200 on account, and that the defendant had supplied the machine nor returned the money.

The defendant pleaded that he never made promise, that the "reasonable time" had not ela and that the plaintiff had not supplied certain draw that he ought to have supplied.

The Jury gave a verdict for the plaintiff—dam £200.

CROWN COURT, MONDAY.

(Before the Lord Chief Baron Pollock.)

THE MURDER AT STUDLEY.

George Gardner, 21, labourer, was placed at the charged with having, on the 23rd of April, 1862, fully murdered Sarah Kirby, his sweetheart, at Stud

The Learned Judge asked the prisoner, when he called on, if he had a Counsel, to which he replied firm voice that he was too poor to employ Counsel. Lordship asked Mr. Stephen to undertake the defe which he immediately consented to do.—Serg O'Brien, with whom was the H. E. C. Leigh, appe for the Crown.

The Learned Sergeant then proceeded to call following evidence:—

George Salt said, he was a labourer, living about yards from Mr. Edge's house. On the 23rd of A last he was employed by Mr. Edge, as was also prisoner. Sarah Kirby was a general domestic serv of Mr. Edge's. On Tuesday night, the 22nd of A he went to the Greyhound Inn, about nine o'cl The prisoner was there, and remained there until in the morning. They left together, at which time prisoner was not drunk or sober. The prisoner rema at his (witness's) cottage until about six on the follow morning.

Charles Russell said that he lived with the pris at Mr. Edge's. He used to be sent by the prisone get beer from Sarah Kirby. Sometimes, when Ki refused, the prisoner said he would murder her, bury her under the turf next minute.

William Bradley, labourer, of Shallowsford, sai Up to September last he was working at Mr. Ed farm. He saw on one occasion that the prisoner pinching and nettling deceased. He told witness t he should like to blow Sarah Kirby's — — brains with a gun. Witness asked him why he should in fere with the girl, telling him that the girl did not w anything to do with him; to which the prisoner rep that witness should never have anything to do with h

Cross-examined — He was a sweetheart of deceased.

Mr. Davis Edge said that he was a farmer, living Outhill, and was the master of the prisoner and Sa Kirby, who had been in his service for twelve mont On one occasion he spoke to the prisoner as to his c duct towards Sarah Kirby, who had complained of h and told him that if it was not discontinued he sho turn him away. Taking the gun employed in the m der in his hand, witness said he usually kept it loaded the parlour of his house. It was loaded on morning of the 23rd of April last. It was loaded w No. 6 shot. On that morning he went to Tamwo Fair. He had given prisoner directions to use the g on that morning. The powder-flask and shot-bag p duced were usually kept in a bureau in his kitchen.

Miss Ann Millet Davis said that she lived with h nephew, and kept his house. She recollected on

THE
BLACK KALENDAR
OF COVENTRY

EDWARD BRADSHAW

The story of Edward 'Duckfat' Bradshaw has become so shrouded in mystery over the thickening mists of time that the truth behind the matter has been lost, and an amusing, romantic myth has replaced it.

Read an account in any book, local newspaper or website, and the modern-day understanding of the case is roughly as follows.

Edward Bradshaw, a young local man apparently known by the unfathomable nickname 'Duckfat', fell in with a gang of thieves who in the early hours of one September morning, 1820, robbed the Malt Shovel public house on Spon End and sat down to enjoy a meal before making off with their loot.

The landlord awoke and went downstairs, only to be murdered by the knife-wielding gang. When the police arrived, they found Bradshaw sitting at a table tucking into a pie.

He went quietly, and it is said that while in the cells at the Police Station on St Mary Street, awaiting his fate, he was regularly sent on errands but always returned, apparently too dim to realise that he was being given a chance to escape.

Bradshaw was executed on Whitley Common, with a crowd of around fifteen thousand people gathering to enjoy the spectacle.

It sounds a fanciful tale, and questions have to be asked. If the landlord was dead, who called the police? Would a young burglar, having just murdered a man in the panic of being disturbed in the still of the night, sit down and eat a pie, no matter how tasty it was?

What is the true story of Edward Bradshaw and the Spon End murder? Read on, dear reader.

*

Edward Bradshaw was the first child born to John Bradshaw, a ribbon weaver, and his wife Elizabeth following their marriage at St Michael's the previous year.[1] The boy was baptised at the same venue on 7 June 1801.[2]

Sisters Hannah (1803) and Elizabeth (1806) quickly arrived, then a seven year gap before Phoebe (1813) and Harriet (1818) joined the Bradshaw clan. Another daughter, Matilda, was born to John and Elizabeth late in 1819.[3]

By this time, only son Edward was approaching his nineteenth birthday. Although there are no records to confirm it, he was probably engaged in the textile industry, prevalent in Coventry in the decades before watchmaking took over, and work undertaken by both his parents and sisters. According to some later newspaper reports, despite the family being poor Edward was fairly well educated, and had attended Bablake School.[4]

By the summer of 1820 Edward had fallen in with a pair of brothers around the same age, John and William Lowe,[5] whose friendship would soon lead to catastrophe.

Between two and three o'clock on the morning of Saturday, 16 September, the youths had broken into the grounds at the rear of the Malt Shovel at 93 Spon End,[6] run by Mrs Sarah Garner,[7] and

1   On 9 July 1800 [England, Select marriages 1538-1973].
2   England, Select Births and Christenings, 1538-1975 [FHL film no. 428986, 428987].
3   Birth and baptism records.
4   *Kenilworth Advertiser*, 29 August 1903.
5   *Birmingham Chronicle*, 5 April 1821.
6   Although the building is undoubtedly older, the first mention of the Malt Shovel dates to around 1800, meaning it had been serving pints for just twenty years at the time of this incident.
7   An advertisement in the *Coventry Herald* of 16 April 1824 reveals that Mrs Garner also owned the large expanse of land now occupied by the car park of the Butts Park Arena.

The Malt Shovel
Courtesy www.HistoricCoventry.co.uk

stole eleven fowls, which were later found in a bag in a nearby field, still alive.

From there, the trio went across to the rear of the Punch Bowl tavern at No. 104, managed by Mr John Bobbett, and entered the kitchen door.[8]

At this point the alarm was sounded, in the form of the dog living next door barking in response to the intruders. Its owner, Mr William Lynes, was woken up and approached his bedroom window.[9] He saw a man carrying a lighted candle emerge from the kitchen of the Punch Bowl and enter the cellar, then reappear and hand something to his companions.

8   The Punch Bowl tavern was closed in 1911. The site is currently occupied by the Rainbow Dragon Chinese takeaway.

9   William Lynes (or Lines) almost certainly lived at 103 Spon End, which later became the long-serving post office. He was at the time of the incident around fifty years old, and a widower. He had been married to second wife Mary for eight years. They had a son, three year old William Jr, and a daughter, Charlotte, aged two.

Spon End, 1887

Arming himself with the first thing which came to hand – a long-handled mop – Mr Lynes went to defend Mr Bobbett's property. Instead of going into his own backyard and confronting the burglars there, he went out his front door and around the Spon End bridge, thereby affording him direct contact in the Punch Bowl grounds.

A journalist from the *Coventry Herald*, writing just six days later, was full of admiration for Mr Lynes as he reported what happened next:

> On his arrival near them, one of the villains exclaimed – "D[amn] your eyes, what do you want!", to which Lynes answered – "One of you, and one I'll have before I go." On this he advanced amid a shower of stones and brickbats, which were thrown at him by the villains, and proceeded fearlessly to the wall which separates Mr B's yard from the brook, in order to secure the person he saw enter the cellar.
>
> The robber, who was armed with a carving knife, cut Mr Lynes dreadfully across the arm, who retaliated by knocking him into the brook with his staff, and then jumped in after him; here a dreadful contest ensured, which was rendered still more unequal by the approach of another of the thieves, who instantly jumped upon Mr L's back. The consequence was, the unfortunate man was dreadfully cut and beat, but he courageously stuck to his man, and with the assistance of Mr J. Eyres, (who fortunately came up to his assistance, and who had been previously engaged with one of the party, but who afterwards escaped), brought the villain (whose name is Bradshaw), in custody to his house.[10]

William Lynes received terrible injuries. He was severely wounded in his face, and a cut on his arm was so deep it was feared he might lose it. His fingers were slashed, as were his legs, and bloodstains on his shirt bore testimony to three deep stab wounds he had received to his torso. It was remarkable that he was still alive; as was the case with Mr Eyres,[11] who had received just one wound – a severe cut on the chin – which, had it been an inch lower, would have surely cut his throat.

10 *Coventry Herald*, 22 September 1820.
11 Possibly the John Eyres born in Coventry in 1790.

The Punch Bowl Tavern (the small building in the centre),
with William Lynes' house next door on the left
Courtesy www.HistoricCoventry.co.uk

In addition to the bag containing Mrs Garner's stolen chickens, police found a stash near the Punch Bowl which revealed the plunder removed from the kitchen before Mr Lynes' intervention: three pairs of boots, a decanter of wine and around thirty shillings, in halfpence pieces. Later recovered was the stolen till, dropped during his flight by the third member of the gang. He, too, was apprehended and taken into custody.[12]

Against John Lowe no evidence could be presented to the magistrates – it was presumably he who had fled the scene and was arrested later, meaning it could not be proved he had been at the scene – but his brother William, and Edward Bradshaw, were committed to trial at the Warwick Lent Assizes.

There, on 5 April 1821, no evidence was produced against William Lowe and he was acquitted. But Edward Bradshaw pleaded Guilty to the charge of burglary, and he was subsequently sentenced to the maximum penalty for that crime – death. Too late for Bradshaw, it wasn't until the Judgement of Death Act of 1823 that a judge could use his discretion as to the death penalty for all crimes except treason and murder, so in 1820 Justice Sir John Richardson had no option but to pass the death sentence upon the young burglar.

The Warrant of Execution, drawn up on 17 April 1821 by Edward Cherry and Kevitt Rotherham, Gentlemen Sheriffs of the City of Coventry, commanded Gaol Keeper Samuel Carter and his officers to

> cause Edward Bradshaw, convicted of Burglary and condemned at the last General Gaol Delivery holden for our said City and County, to be hanged till he is dead on Wednesday the eighteenth day of April instant, pursuant two the sentence passed upon him.[13]

The location was to be Whitley Common, a mile from the city centre, which at that time was often used for executions. There

---

12 *Coventry Herald*, 22 September 1820.
13 Execution warrant of Edward Bradshaw [Coventry Archives: BA/E/11/114/109].

waiting – some for many hours to ensure a good view – was a crowd estimated at upwards of fifteen thousand.

Also in attendance were a large number of reporters, one of whom captured the grim proceedings in solemn detail:

> Considerable interest was excited, as no similar event had taken place in the City or its neighbourhood for the last 21 years. During his confinement after condemnation, the unhappy man was visited by a number of Ministers and pious persons. He sometimes discovered a pentinent spirit, and seemed humbled on account of his transgressions; but these impressions were but occasional and of short duration.

> Early on the morning of his execution, he was visited by several Ministers. When the summons came for him to repair to the fatal spot, he discovered no kind of hesitation or reluctance. He walked from the prison yard into the County Hall, where, having been pinioned, he was conducted from thence in a coach to the place of execution, where he arrived about a quarter past eleven o'clock.

> As he passed through the crowd to the place of execution, his attention appeared to be more interested in the number of persons assembled together, and in recognising some of his old companions, than in his own unhappy condition; and it was with difficulty that the Ministers with him could fix his attention on a Bible which he held in his hand.

> He ascended the scaffold with a firm step. He was there attended by the Rev Messrs Hughes, Thomson, Franklin and Sibree. After a Psalm had been sung and a prayer offered, Bradshaw requested that he might address the spectators. He confessed himself Guilty of the crime for which he suffered, and acknowledged the justice of his sentence, and several times earnestly entreated those who saw him, and particularly his old companions, to take warning by his unhappy fate; not to violate the Sabbath, nor to associate with evil company, which two things, he said, had brought him to his untimely end.

> The Rev Mr Hughes then, at the request of Bradshaw, delivered a most appropriate and impressive address to the multitude; after which, Bradshaw knelt down on the scaffold and prayed in a very audible voice and impressive manner. Having concluded his prayer, he took leave of those who surrounded him, and a few

minutes before 12 o'clock was launched into eternity.[14]

After hanging for an hour, as prescribed by law, the body of Edward Bradshaw was cut down and removed back to County Hall. Four days later he was buried at the 'new burying ground' of St Michael's – where he had been baptised just twenty short years earlier.[15]

*

Bradshaw's parents both died in 1842, both aged sixty-five. His eldest sister, Hannah, had already passed away, unmarried, in 1831. She was just twenty-eight years old. Younger siblings Phoebe and Harriett married and lived long lives, both passing away in their seventies in the 1890s.

Youngest sister Matilda Bradshaw had four children, born between 1860 and 1866. All were baptised on 21 January 1870, with no father named. However, following the birth of the youngest, Elizabeth, the court issued a bastardy order against one Francis Bates, a young weaver. He and Matilda eventually married in 1891, and were still together at the time of the 1911 Census twenty years later.[16]

William and John Lowe appear to have heeded Bradshaw's warning, for they never again appeared before the magistrates.

Joseph Bobbett, landlord of the Punch Bowl, did not let the burglary and attack on his Good Samaritan neighbour scare him from the tavern; he remained behind the bar for another decade, until he was declared bankrupt in April 1830.[17] The following year, the Punch Bowl was embroiled in an even more notorious case when a woman named Mary Ann Southam testified at the inquest into the death of William Higgins that she had been drinking at the tavern with Mary Ann, his nineteen year old niece, on the afternoon he died.[18] Mary Ann Higgins was later arrested and convicted of

14   *Staffordshire Advertiser*, 28 April 1821.
15   Burial records of the Parish of St Michael.
16   Birth and baptism records; 1911 Census.
17   *Perry's Bankrupt Gazette*, 10 April 1830.
18   *Coventry Herald*, 1 April 1831.

his murder by poisoning; she was the last woman hanged in public at Coventry.

William Lynes, despite his horrific injuries, survived the assault by Edward Bradshaw and no doubt became something of a local celebrity. He died at his home on Spon Street nearly a quarter of a century later in 1843, at the grand age of seventy-one.[19]

It was probably just as well. The have-a-go hero would have been deeply disappointed by his son William Jr, who in 1848 found himself before magistrates following a series of thefts. Now aged thirty-two, he had been employed by Rotherhams, the city's pre-eminent watchmaking firm, for seventeen years, since becoming an apprentice there. Desperate for money, he had stolen three gold watches from his place of work and sold the cases to receiver James Sanders. The inner parts of the watches he had thrown into the Coventry canal. Admitting his guilt and turning Queen's Evidence against Sanders William avoided a sentence,[20] but lost his employment at one of the the most respected of all Coventry businesses, his name and reputation in the dirt. His father would have turned in his grave.

*

So, there we have it. No murder, no errands run from the prison cells – and no pie. And regarding the moniker 'Duckfat' – the earliest mention I can find of that comes from the *Kenilworth Advertiser* of 9 January 1897 – seventy-seven years after the incident. It's quite possible that he was indeed known by that name, but it's strange that there are no mentions in the press closer in time to the event.

The *Kenilworth Advertiser* piece also claims, intriguingly, that Bradshaw requested the journey from County Hall to Whitley Common be halted as it passed the Horse and Jockey public house on Much Park Street as he saw his former companions standing outside, and wished to warn them to mend their ways.

19 Burial record of William Lines, on 4 October 1843 at St Michael's.
20 *Coventry Standard*, 7 January 1848.

But, equally, the article incorrectly mentions that the condemned man was convicted of 'cutting and wounding the landlord' – although the same newspaper did correct the claim in their edition of 29 August 1903, by stating that Bradshaw had in fact cut and wounded Mr Lynes, who had gone to the landlord's assistance.

It goes to show how a juicy story can be twisted, added to and adapted as time passes. And in the case of Duckfat Bradshaw, the truth is as remarkable as the myth.

SUSANNAH JARVIS

Close by the Coventry Canal Basin, the Canal Tavern on Leicester Row no doubt saw a lot of trade from those working on the water. It first appears in records in 1835, as a beer house, with Robert Golsby named as the 'beer retailer'.[21] The inn quickly gained its licenced name, but the Canal Tavern soon after appeared in local newspapers for less than desirable reasons.

On 19 June 1838 a nineteen year old weaver named John Taylor entered the premises and ordered a pint of ale, and two pennyworth of bread and cheese. Mrs Golsby served him, and brought him a knife with which to cut his supper.

Half an hour later Taylor left, and on clearing up Robert Golsby realised that the knife was missing. Constable James Smith happened to be passing, so the landlord told him what had happened and the officer was able to chase the young drinker. When he was within two or three yards of him PC Smith saw Taylor throw the knife away. The policeman brought both thief and knife back to the Canal Tavern, where Golsby identified the item.

At the Police Court hearing on 6 July, despite claiming he had never had bread and cheese at the hostelry in question, and the Bench hearing references as to his good character from his friends Jonathan Fitzpatrick and John Horton, Taylor was found Guilty

21   *Pigot & Co.'s Directory of Warwickshire*, 1835.

and sentenced to six months with hard labour.[22]

It would not be the last time police would be called to the Canal Tavern.

*

Landlord Robert Golsby had been born in Thorpe Mandeville, Northamptonshire in September 1807. He married Susan Wilson at St Martin's, Birmingham in 1833 and the couple soon welcomed a daughter, Ann. The following year they moved into the Canal Tavern, and another daughter, Mary, was born there in 1840. A third daughter, Emma, arrived at the end of 1842.[23]

Almost eighteen months later, in the spring of 1844, the family were enjoying life. Mr and Mrs Golsby continued to run the busy Canal Tavern, and had employed a young nursemaid to help look after baby Emma.

Susannah Jarvis had been born at Kenilworth to John, a comb maker, and his wife Mary in 1830.[24] She was just thirteen years old when taken on by the Golsbys, and her duties were to walk, dress and generally care for little Emma, a role she had carried out for seven months.[25]

Monday, 22 April 1844 started as any other day. Robert Golsby busied himself in the pub, preparing for what he hoped would be a profitable day.

The area around the Canal Basin was a hive of activity, and the streets were thronged with people going about their business.

That afternoon a man named William Carter, who lived on Leicester Street to the rear of the Canal Tavern from which a passage gave access to inn, saw a man going backwards and forwards around the street several times, with his head down as though looking for something. At one point he picked up a piece of orange peel and

22 *Coventry Standard*, 6 July 1838.
23 Baptism and marriage records.
24 Baptism record of Susannah Jarvis.
25 The *Coventry Herald* of 26 April 1844 states in their coverage of the inquest that Susannah had been employed by the Golsbys since "Michaelmas last", ie September 1843.

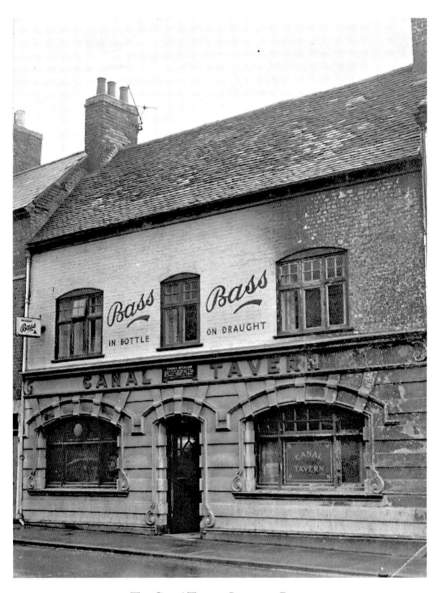

The Canal Tavern, Leicester Row
Courtesy www.HistoricCoventry.co.uk

ate it. Mr Carter saw that, unusually, the man was without shoes or socks.

At quarter to seven Mrs Eliza Harvey was returning home from work and had just got to the Cranes Inn, a hundred yards from the Canal Tavern, when she encountered a man walking up from Bishop Street. He was wearing a light-coloured jacket, rounded at the hem, and was barefoot.

Fifteen minutes later a barefooted man was seen walking on Leicester Street near the junction with Tower Street by Mrs Ann Watson.

At eight o'clock, Thomas King saw a man sitting on the bank of the footpath by Radford Road, a quarter of a mile from the Canal Tavern. He had no shoes on, and had his head down, looking at his hands.

A man named Thomas Glenn had enjoyed two halves of ale at the Holly Bush on Cook Street, having entered the pub as the church bell struck seven o'clock. On leaving, he made his way along Leicester Street and into Leicester Row, heading for his home in Foleshill. As he passed the rear of the Canal Tavern he saw a man without shoes coming out of the passage; he was unable to say exactly what time it was, but later estimated it was between 7.45 and 8.00pm.

Were all these sightings of the same man?

At the Canal Tavern, at around the time the mysterious bare-footed man was spotted by various witnesses, Mrs Susan Golsby was putting her middle daughter Mary to bed. She was now four years old. Mrs Golsby had already placed baby Emma in her cradle, which stood in the back kitchen downstairs, taking off her socks and covering her with a blanket. She then washed Mary in the same back kitchen then took her upstairs to get her ready for bed, leaving nursemaid Susannah to watch over the infant. Nine year old Ann was watching the empty bar, in the absence of her father. Her mother gave her a cake, and Ann began combing her hair. She ventured to the front door of the tavern to see if any of her playmates were around, but never set foot outside.

As she stood there, Susannah Jarvis appeared on the steps into

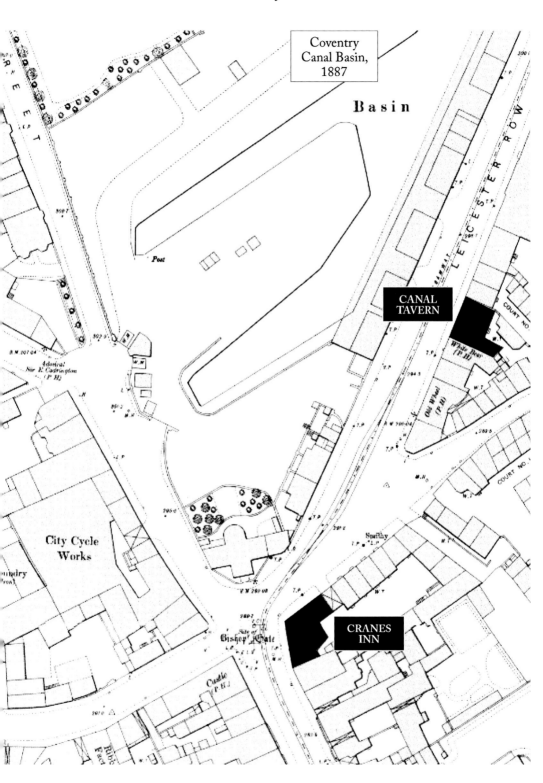

Coventry
Canal Basin,
1887

B a s i n

LEICESTER ROW

CANAL
TAVERN

City Cycle
Works

CRANES
INN

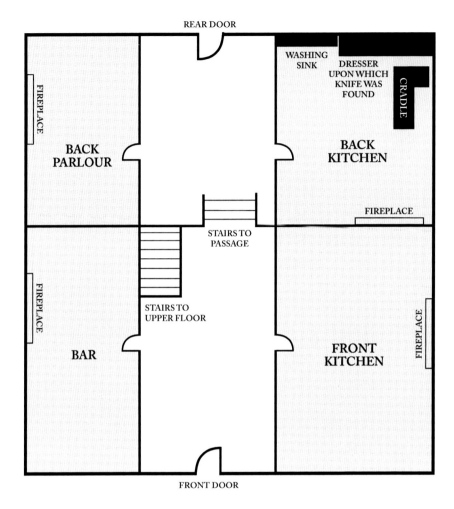

Plan of the Canal Tavern

the passage leading from the back kitchen and said she was going to the outside privy. Ann went back into the bar and laid down the comb she had been using, but no sooner had she done so than a strange kind of scream came from the back kitchen; Ann would later tell the inquest it sounded like a 'growling' kind of noise, being emitted five or six times.[26]

Mrs Golsby, putting Mary to bed, had also heard the cries, and called out asking what was the matter. After receiving no reply,

26 *Coventry Herald*, 9 August 1844.

she ran downstairs. Before she reached the bottom of the stairs, Susannah Jarvis cried out, "A man has killed the baby, and has run down the yard!"

Understandably alarmed, Mrs Golsby rushed to the cradle to check on her daughter. She found Emma breathing in laboured gasps, her head and chest covered in blood. Screaming "Murder!", the horror-stricken mother snatched up the infant and ran to the front door, bursting into the busy street. Passers-by rushed to her aid, and a doctor and police were both summoned. Sadly, before they arrived little Emma Golsby was dead.

Just four minutes had elapsed between Mrs Golsby placed Emma in the cradle, and coming back downstairs to find her daughter covered in blood.[27]

PC Edmund Salmon arrived, and first examined the cradle. The pillow and bedclothes were saturated with blood. Nearby, on the dresser, were streaks of blood where a carving knife had been placed.

Dr Overton arrived and examined the body of the infant, noting that there was a wound at the base of the neck, on the left side, which had been caused by a single stab. He did not think there would be any spurting of the blood, the carotid artery not having been punctured. There were a few small spots of blood on the wall close to where the cradle stood.

Inspector Vice arrived and examined the yard and passages, but found nothing untoward.

Susannah Jarvis' clothes were scrutinised, and it was observed that her pinafore appeared crumpled at the middle, with a few spots of blood, and there were more on the bottom of her dress.

She repeated her story to the inspector, saying that she had been in the privy when she heard the baby scream. On coming out she saw a tall man without shoes or socks emerge from the back kitchen door. As Susannah went back into the room, Mrs Golsby arrived and lifted Emma from the cradle.

This chimed with the sightings of such a man over the previous few

---

27 *Coventry Herald*, 26 April 1844.

hours, but when Inspector Vice made enquiries at the properties immediately adjoining the Canal Tavern, nobody seemed to have observed a bare-footed man in the minutes before the murder.

Mrs Golsby told a very different story.

While baby Emma had been happy enough in Susannah's company at first, although not especially fond of her, she had recently taken a great aversion to the girl.

Soon after starting her employment the new nursemaid had shaken the baby, but having been scolded for doing so had not been known to do it again. But on the Friday before the murder, at around six o'clock in the evening, Mrs Golsby had washed the infant around the face and neck and told Susannah to take her out for a walk. An hour later they returned, and the nurse undressed the baby and put her in the cradle. Suddenly Mrs Golsby heard her daughter cry out, and on investigating saw marks around her neck as if she had been pinched or scratched. Susannah Jarvis said she knew nothing about the marks.

The following day Emma displayed even greater reluctance to go to the nurse, so Susannah was put to other work and the baby was looked after by the Golsbys' other servant, Maria Fowkes.

On the Monday morning Mrs Golsby decided she had to do something. In earshot of Susannah Jarvis, she instructed Maria Fowkes to go and see the girl's parents at Kenilworth, and tell them that unless things improved within the next week she would be sending their daughter home. This was done, Mrs Golsby told police, in the hope that Susannah would mend her ways.

Later that day, when Mrs Golsby had heard the strange cries coming from downstairs, she had left middle daughter Mary on the floor of the bedroom and run downstairs, arriving at the back kitchen in time to see Susannah Jarvis just leaving the cradle, about a yard and a half away from it.

Mrs Golsby asked, "What's the matter?," and was told that a man had either killer or stabbed the baby – she couldn't remember the wording the nursegirl had used.

She asked Susannah what had happened next.

"Where's the man gone?"

"Down the yard."

"No, it's no man – it's you I doubt."

This revelation cast a dark shadow over Susannah Jarvis, and she taken into custody.

Overnight, the rumour mill rumbled on. Had the infant been murdered by the girl in whose care she had been entrusted, or had the strange barefooted man carried out the deed. If so, what was his motive? Another theory was that the death had been caused by Ann Golsby, playing at 'sticking pigs' with her baby sister.

The inquest before Coroner W.H. Seymour was held over the following two evenings, on 23 and 24 April, and at the Wheel Tavern, also on Leicester Row, and just three doors along from the scene of the murder. The jury consisted of local men from honest occupations, including two bakers, a wheelwright and a boatmaker. They would surely exercise their worldly common sense when assessing the evidence.[28]

There was naturally a lot of local excitement in proceedings, and reporters took great interest in Susannah, with one commenting:

> The conduct of the prisoner on the first evening, we were pained to observe, was far from becoming. She is a thin, and rather agreeable, sharp-looking country girl; but her demeanour on this occasion evinced a trifling indifference, and almost pertness, totally incompatible with the horrifying case with which she was so intimately connected. Innocence, it might have been thought, would have been indicated by something like sympathy and feelings of emotion for the stressing fate of the murdered babe she had so long nursed; while guilt was likely to have be betrayed by a speaking countenance, or an agitated frame; but neither one not the other of any of these symptoms did she manifest. On Wednesday evening, however, her manners were considerably altered, and she seemed faint, dispirited, and restless, though by no means unconscious of what was passing.[29]

28 *Coventry Herald*, 26 April 1844.
29 *Coventry Herald*, 26 April 1844.

Despite evidence from Kenilworth's Rev Parry and schoolmistress Mrs Swaine bearing testimony of the girl's good character, the evidence given by Dr John Overton as to the wounds inflicted on poor Emma Golsby no doubt weighed heavy in the thoughts of the jury:

> The wound was about an inch and a half long, and gaped about an inch and a quarter wide. The knife was penetrated just about the sternum, or breast-bone; and being driven in an oblique direction, it severed the jugular vein, separated the carotid artery, wounded a portion of the lungs, and entered the chest; it terminated its course at the posterior part of the body, between the fourth and fifth ribs, almost perforating the skin on the outside, making the depth of it betwixt fie and six inches.[30]

It's almost needless to say that Susannah Jarvis was committed to trial.

The reporter from the *Warwick Advertiser*, reporting on the inquest, was forthright in his horror at the girl's conduct, not bothering to wait for the actual trial before condemning her:

> The unnatural young wretch was brought before the inquest in custody, and after the verdict of the jury she was committed to gaol for trial on the charge of murder. She heard the verdict unmoved; and when she parted from her father and mother (who were present), they gave proof that their wretched child had been trained in the school of depravity; for, in the hearing of the jury and people in attendance, they advised her, at the time of parting, to refuse to eat or drink in prison, whoever might offer it to her, but to pine herself to death! …Perhaps, altogether, this is the most frightful and heart-chilling instance of youthful brutality and cold-blooded cruelty that has ever been recorded in the annals of crime in this country.

The Summer Warwickshire Assizes opened on Monday, 5 August 1844. The trial of Susannah Jarvis was set for the following day, and began at nine o'clock in the morning.

---

30   *Warwick Advertiser*, 27 April 1844.

Newspaper reporters confirmed that, as would be expected, the courtroom was packed with spectators, mostly "of a highly respectable and well-dressed class of persons... The upper gallery was almost exclusively filled by ladies."

Evidence was given by a number of witnesses, mostly repeating the testimony given at the inquest, but the prosecution had brought forward a number of witnesses to show that Susannah Jarvis' story of a man entering the passage, killing the baby and then escaping by the same route was entirely untrue.

One man, John Griffin, stated that he had been standing at his door on Leicester Street, which overlooked the back passage of the Canal Tavern, when the cry of murder had been raised, and had not seen anyone of in or come out. On hearing the screams of Mrs Golsby he had raced to the back kitchen, where he saw a craving knife wet with blood lying on the dresser near the cradle.

The defending counsel, Mr Humfries, reminded the jury of the seriousness of their decision. A Guilty verdict, he said, would mean the hanging of a young girl. He told them that the small scratches on the infant's neck found on the Friday evening might have been caused by a pin, and the minute spots of blood on Susannah's pinafore could have been deposited there in the confusion caused by the discovery of the murder. All the evidence against the defendent was, he told them, entirely circumstantial.

Judge Mr Justice Coleman then began his summing up. He reminded the jury that the law stated children under seven years old were not held responsible for any offence they might commit; above fourteen they were considered responsible, and between seven and fourteen their responsibility was determined by the degree of intelligence displayed. He spoke of the improbability of the defendant's claim of a man entering the back kitchen, but on the other hand reminded the jury that such a man had indeed been seen in the vicinity in the hours leading up to the murder. His summing up concluded at 5.35pm, after an hour and twenty minutes.

While a jury would often agree their decision without leaving the box, on this occasion it was clear that a unanimous verdict would not be arrived at quickly, and after a quarter of an hour they requested they be allowed to retire to discuss the evidence more fully.

The jury was still in discussion when the court closed for the evening, so were forced to remain in custody overnight. At half past six the following morning Mr Justice Coleman visited them with bread and water, and court resumed at ten o'clock. The jury had not, however reached a unanimous decision, and told the Clerk of Arraigns that it was impossible they would.

With no alternative, Mr Justice Coleman ordered them to be discharged, and that the prisoner be remanded in custody until the next Assizes, when a new trial would be held.

Susannah Jarvis sat through the two days bearing a calm and indifferent demeanour, and showed no emotion at the order for her to be detained until the next Assizes.[31]

The girl would endure remaining in custody for seven months, awaiting her second visit to the dock. The Spring Assizes opened on Thursday, 27 March 1845, by which time she had turned fourteen years old, and thus entirely accountable for her actions; she would see the hangman's noose should she be found Guilty.

The day began in an unusual fashion, with Mr Justice Maule complaining about the deplorable state of Coventry. Before discharging the Grand Jury, who had passed a true bill on all the trials to be heard at the Assizes, the *Coventry Herald* reported how Mr Justice Maule

> said there was one subject to which he thought he ought to direct their attention before they left; it was as to the sanitary condition of the town, for he believed Coventry was one of the most unhealthy places in England, and in his opinion this was confirmed by the sort of lodgings provided for the Judges; for as soon as he entered the house, he could not help but be struck with the intolerable stench which met him, and the Sherriff was equally struck by the same fact; and it was same upstairs as down; indeed, the stench was so abominable, that he found it impossible to remain, for had he done so, being not in a very

31 *Coventry Herald*, 9 August 1844.

good state of health, it would have been death to him. It was attempted to account for this abominable stench this morning by saying it arose from a mouldy carpet; but that could not be – that was not the cause, but the effect. He mentioned this matter not from any individual feeling in particular with regard to himself, but out of regard to the general health of the town, and especially for the sake of the poor people who resided it, for he certainly considered it to be the duty of gentlemen of wealth and station like the Grand Jury to try to do something in their day and generation, with a view of getting such as state of things altered as that which he had described.

With the members of the Grand Jury thus being sent away with a flea in their ear, and no doubt going to inspect to carpets of Coventry, it was time to get down to the matter in hand – the trial of Susannah Jarvis for the murder of Emma Golsby.

Evidence heard was much the same as the earlier trial, but excitement was caused by a scale model of the Canal Tavern and its environs being produced, in order to aid the jury to ascertain for themselves exactly what could and could not be seen from the vantage points of the various witnesses.

They were also able to examine the prisoner's dress and pinafore, and view the small spots of blood upon them.

Mr Humfrey, once again defending, told the jury that the position of the spots of blood on the wall, four feet above the cradle, indicated they had dripped from the knife used to murder the poor child, which must therefore have been held by a person taller than the prisoner. He reminded them that throughout her long incarceration Susannah Jarvis had not once wavered from her story, or altered it in any way.

In summing up, Mr Justice Maule appeared to favour the evidence for the prisoner, rather than against, and in complete contrast to their counterparts the previous August, this time the jury took just twenty minutes to find Susannah Jarvis Not Guilty. At half past four on Thursday, 27 March 1845 she walked free from the court.[32]

The murder of Emma Golsby has never been solved.

32 *Coventry Herald*, 9 August 1844.

*

Understandably, grieving father Robert Golsby and his family could not stay on long at the Canal Tavern. In fact, a report of the first trial in August 1844 – four months after the murder – describes him as 'late of the Canal Tavern', indicating he had almost immediately vacated the premises.

In February 1847, less than two years after the loss of Emma, he had moved to the Cranes Inn – close by, on Bishop Street – taking over the licence from William Conway.[33] Another daughter, Elizabeth, was born there in 1848.

The census of 1851 shows that the family were still at the Cranes; in addition, Robert appears to have been earning extra income at this time by operating as a salt merchant. Both an advertisement for the sale of a salt warehouse in 1848,[34] and the *Coventry Directory* of 1850, list him as working on the premises. The family seemed to be getting on with their lives.

But over the next two years things went wrong.

Magistrates sitting to hear a charge against cattle dealer William Pickering in April 1852 heard that the long-running nuisance of the cattle market around the junction of Radford Road, Leicester Row and Bishop Street had driven one local businessman to distraction, prompting a constable on duty at the market to step in:

> Collis, the Policeman, made a statement to the Magistrates of the way in which he had been treated by Mr Golsby, the landlord of the Cranes Inn. A drover had driven a herd of beasts on to the footway by the side of the Cranes Inn, and he desired the man to drive his cattle off. The drover refused to do so, and he (Collis) accordingly drove the cattle off. Mr Golsby, however, rushed out in a furious passion, and drove the beasts back again upon the footpath, using the foulest language, and declaring that both the Police and the Magistrates were fools; and that he would not be robbed of his custom by having the cattle driven off the

---

33 *Coventry Herald*, 26 February 1847. The Poor Rate payment book for that year records Robert Golsby as a victualler on Bishop Street.
34 *Coventry Herald*, 7 April 1848.

footpath. The Magistrates declared that note might be taken of Mr Golsby's conduct, to be referred to at the next licensing day.[35]

Sure enough, repercussions came the first opportunity afford to the magistrates, in April 1853, and the licence was taken off Golsby and transferred to Elizabeth Wright.[36]

He had already been prepared; an advertisement placed by auctioneers Brown and Clarke announced the sale of the contents of the Cranes the month before Golsby's licence was ended, with all the brewing equipment, casks and glasses on offer – even the Golsbys' bedroom furniture was included in the sale. The emptied building was then intended to be let as a house.[37] In the event, although Robert Golsby vacated the premises the Cranes remained in business.

A few weeks later a notice by Mr Holt, solicitor, dated 20 April 1853, appeared in local newspapers which laid bare the sad state of affairs:

> Whereas a Petition of Robert Golsby, now and for five weeks past at lodgings at No. 2, Park Side, Coventry, in the County of Warwick, out of business; and previously, and for six years of Bishop Street, Coventry aforesaid, Innkeeper, Livery Stable Keeper, Dealer in Tobacco, Salt, Hay, Straw, and Corn, an Insolvent Debtor, having been filed in the County Court of Warwickshire, to be holden at Coventry… the said Robert Golsby is hereby required to appear in the said Court, before the Judge of the said Court, on the Thirtieth day of May, 1853, at Twelve o'Clock at Noon precisely, for his First Examination touching his Debts, Estate, and Effects, and to be further dealt with according to the provisions of the said Statutes.[38]

It was a further hurtful blow for a hard-working man, who just eight years earlier had lost a much-loved child in the most tragic of circumstances, and for which no-one had been held accountable.

35   *Coventry Herald*, 23 April 1852.
36   *Coventry Standard*, 8 April 1853.
37   *Coventry Standard*, 25 February 1853.
38   *Coventry Herald*, 29 April 1853.

But life must go on. In 1860 another daughter, Fanny, was born – no doubt a surprise to her parents, who were now fifty-three and forty-eight. The census of the following year recorded the family at 61 New Street, with Robert now earning a living as a porter.

*

Robert Golsby died on 11 January 1873, at the relatively young age of sixty-one. He was buried at Holy Trinity Churchyard, where wife Susan joined him in 1882.[39] The headstone bearing their names today lies flat on the south side of the churchyard, opposite the Turtle Bay restaurant.

The two elder sisters of poor murdered Emma went on to live long lives.

Mary, just four years old and being put to bed by her mother when her infant sister drew her last breath, remained unmarried and died at Coventry Workhouse in 1911, at the aged of seventy-two.[40]

Ann, at ten left at the bar of the Canal Tavern and who almost certainly witnessed the murder of baby Emma, married widowed hairdresser John Goldsby at Holy Trinity on Boxing Day 1872; Mary was one of the witnesses. The groom was forty years old, the bride thirty-seven. Both were living at New Street at the time of the marriage.[41]

Despite not being in the first flush of youth, the couple soon welcomed a daughter, Gertrude, and a son, Lionel, joined the family in 1880. John was running a barber's shop,[42] and in time his son would join him in the business.[43]

Ann Goldsby died in 1909, aged seventy-four.

*

What of Susannah Jarvis, the young girl who stood trial for the

---

39   Dates from headstone.
40   Death record of Mary Wilson Golsby.
41   Marriage certificate of John Goldsby and Anne Golsby.
42   1881 Census.
43   1891 Census.

murder of little Emma Golsby?

Following her acquittal she continued to live at her parents' home at Kenilworth, on New Row, near the castle.[44] On Christmas Day, nine months after the trial, the Jarvis family gathered at Kenilworth's parish church to celebrate the marriage of Susannah's elder sister Ann to local comb maker Edward James. Over the next two decades the couple would welcome ten children.

On 13 August 1854, at twenty-five years old, Susannah married George Barber, a labourer. She signed the certificate with an 'X'.[45] They too would enjoy a large family, with nine children coming along over the years.

By the time of the 1861 Census the family had settled at Clinton Lane, leading to Kenilworth castle, and what would prove to be their long-running home. George was working as an agricultural labourer, and Susannah a 'field woman'. It was work no doubt carried out by the majority of Kenilworth residents at the time, and their sons would follow the same path. Even at the age of seventy-four,[46] the year before his death,[47] George was still labouring.

His widow Susannah lived a further fourteen years. The census of 1911 records her as living alone at 111 Clinton Lane; an address she had known for fifty years. Interestingly, Susannah was able to sign the return, indicating that at some point since her wedding she had learned to write. She was now eighty-one, with seven of her nine children still living.

She eventually passed away four years later, in 1916.[48] Did saddened friends and neighbours, no doubt mourning the loss of a lady who had been a member of the community for so long, know of her brush with the law all those years earlier?

In her final days, did Susannah Jarvis think of her weeks as a young girl employed by the Golsby family? Only she knew the

44 1851 Census.
45 Marriage certificate of George Barber and Susannah Jarvis.
46 1901 Census.
47 George Barber was buried at Kenilworth on 18 September 1902.
48 Death record of Susannah Barber, Q1 1916.

Clinton Lane, Kenilworth. Could one of the women leaning over the fence be
Susannah Barber, and are her children amongst those in the foreground?

truth of the horrible death of baby Emma, a secret she took to her
grave.

Reviewing the evidence, in all probability it seems likely that she
was indeed the culprit. Yes, a rough-looking, bare-footed man had
been seen in the area around the Canal Tavern in the hours before
the murder, but in my opinion Susannah Jarvis carried out a terrible
punishment on a child she had taken an intense dislike to, and
blamed the deed on the bare-foot man that she had also seen that
afternoon; a man who was, in all likelihood, simply an innocent
down-at-heel traveller.

NOVEMBER 1859

JOHN KINGTON

The murder of a child is without doubt the worst experience a mother will have to endure. Close behind this is an infant being orphaned through the loss of its mother, as was the case in our next story; the murder of a young woman, her baby just nineteen months old, horribly slain by her estranged husband.

Elizabeth Ann Holmes had been the first child born to Samuel and Elizabeth Sr, in 1838, and six siblings soon followed. Samuel was a constable in the Coventry City Police Force, his name regularly appearing in local newspaper reports of magistrates' hearings over the years, such as the following arrest in September 1840:

> Sarah Langford, the keeper of a brothel in Dead Lane, was brought up by Samuel Holmes, who gave a most disgusting account of the wretched and filthy state of her house, and the manner in which she harboured young girls for prostitution, one of whom he brought to the [Police] office with him. She was reprimanded and discharged.[49]

It's easy to imagine Samuel Holmes extending a protective arm around his daughters, knowing the horrors in the world which awaited those who took the wrong path.

But by the time of the 1851 Census things had gone wrong.

49 *Coventry Standard*, 2 October 1840. Dead Lane was more formerly known as St John Street, which runs between Little Park Street and Much Park Street.

Samuel was now working as hand loom silk weaver, his career with the Police brought to an abrupt halt. A later newspaper report claimed that he had been discharged for drunkenness on duty,[50] and the final mention of him in relation to Police duties came in August 1849.

The 1851 record shows the family living on Primrose Hill Terrace, with both parents and elder children engaged in the weaving trade. Elizabeth was occupied as a filler.

Further tragedy struck when mother Elizabeth Sr died, on 26 April 1854, aged just thirty-nine.[51]

If reports following her death are to be believed, soon after her mother's death Elizabeth Jr met a carpenter and became pregnant; he absconded to Birmingham, but the infant died at an early age.[52]

As if her troubles weren't already great enough, Elizabeth then met John Kington.

He was a few months older than her, having been baptised at Coventry's St John the Baptist on 15 May 1837. The census of 1851 shows fourteen year old John working as a weaver, as were his parents John Sr and Hannah, and twelve year old sister Sarah. The youngest children – Thomas, Charlotte and William – were all at school. The Kington family was at this time living on Whitefriars Lane.

Young John Kington then joined the 1st Warwick Militia as a drummer, but was rejected on medical grounds due to his suffering fits. By all accounts he had acquired a reputation as a petty thief, and a man of short temper.

He met Elizabeth Holmes, and the pair lodged together at a house on Mill Lane, which provided fuel for the gossip mongers. Supposedly to "stop the reports",[53] the couple married at St Michael's on 5 April 1858 – Easter Monday – both aged twenty.[54]

---

50 *Coventry Standard*, 19 November 1859.
51 *Coventry Standard*, 28 April 1854.
52 *Coventry Standard*, 19 November 1859.
53 *Coventry Standard*, 19 November 1859.
54 Marriage certificate of John Kington and Elizabeth Ann Holmes.

But the rumour mill had been right all along; their daughter, Martha Elizabeth Kington, was born just over three weeks later on 29 April.[55]

A later report spelled out the nature of their unhappy marriage, perhaps exaggerating the personalities of both husband and wife:

> No doubt the miserable man was, according to his nature, strongly attached to his wife; so strongly, that out of his very attachment rose the feelings which led him to put an end to her existence. He is not to be looked upon as a man who had any yearnings for pure domestic happiness. His wife was to be his obedient and willing slave, when required to earn means for their mutual subsistence, to fall in with his desires, and, in return, thankfully to receive that surly treatment which alone his churlish nature could give.

> That this particular woman should be his wife, and on these terms, became so strong a passion as to make its gratification essential to his very existence. On the other hand, the poor woman seems to have been a commonplace person, without any peculiar personal attractions, and with neither very strong feelings or great intellect, incapable of appreciating a strong attachment in anyone, or understanding that any such could exist accompanied by rude and brutal treatment towards its object. Most likely, whatever regard she may have had towards her husband, was alienated by his behaviour, and she began to show indifference, and a return of ill temper; visits and complaints to her father followed, and frequent family quarrels were the result.[56]

The ill-tempered couple lived with baby Martha in a yard in Freeth Street, and afterwards on East Street. Kington tired of their life at this point, and sold the best of their meagre possessions then went to London. Elizabeth took the baby and the rest of their belongings to her father's house, which was by this time on Well Street.

Kington returned to Coventry in June 1849 and took up lodgings at the home of Mr and Mrs Thornett, above their butcher's shop

---

55 Baptism record of Martha Kington.
56 *Coventry Standard*, 19 November 1859.

at 37 Freeth Street.[57] He persuaded Elizabeth to join him, which she did against her better judgement – and no doubt advice of her father – but the same old arguments soon broke out. With his wife now back under his control, Kington's behaviour worsened.

> His conduct, previously bad enough, now became terrible – in fact the woman was so brutally ill-used that is was necessary to procure medical advice, and Mr Dresser attended her. Knives and razors were brandished before her while in bed, and threats of that which has so fearfully come to pass were savagely uttered.
>
> Under these circumstances she left her lodgings, in company of a policeman, and stayed a night with her relatives. Next morning, at the request of her father, a policeman was ordered by the magistrates to escort the woman along the streets, in order that she might apply for a warrant for her husband's apprehension, her fears of him not allowing her to stir abroad alone.[58]

John Kington was accordingly brought before the magistrates, but his cool demeanour before the Bench confirmed his indifference to the nature of the charge, firmly believing he was in his rights to treat his wife however he deemed fit. He was bound over to keep the peace for three months, but in the absence of a surety being paid – his own father wanting nothing to do with him – Kington was sent to gaol for six weeks.

While he was serving his sentence, Elizabeth continued to live at Mrs Thornett's, and found a job at Eli Green's weaving factory on East Street., earning ten shillings a week. Baby Martha was sent to a nurse, and the only visitor Elizabeth admitted was her brother, Walter.

When John Kington was released he immediately went to Freeth Street and attempted to persuade his wife to allow him to live with her again; she flat refused, and he was forced to stay at his father's house. On Friday 11 November he followed her to Samuel Holmes' house, where an almighty row broke out and a final refusal from

---

57 Inquest testimony of Ann Thornett, as reported in the *Coventry Standard* of 19 November 1859.

58 *Coventry Standard*, 19 November 1859.

Elizabeth was delivered. John Kingston appears to have finally accepted her decision – but she was to pay for it with her life.

When John Kington was released he immediately went to Freeth Street and attempted to persuade his wife to allow him to live with her again; she flat refused, and he was forced to stay at his father's house. On Friday 11 November he followed her to Samuel Holmes' house, where an almighty row broke out and a final refusal from Elizabeth was delivered. John Kingston appears to have finally accepted her decision – but she was to pay for it with her life.

*

Elizabeth woke early on the morning of Saturday, 12 November. Although she had work that day, she helped Mrs Thornett with the household chores, then prepared herself breakfast which she took with her to her father's house on Jordan Well, leaving her lodgings on Freeth Street at 6.45am.

Since her husband's release from prison she had planned on being escorted to work by her brother Walter, so fearful was she that John Kington would make an appearance.

She arrived at the family home around seven o'clock and, leaving the breakfast parcel there with the intention of returning to eat around half past eight, left the house with Walter. Heading along Far Gosford Street, they got as far as Read's factory before Elizabeth's fears were realised.

A reporter from the *Coventry Standard* later described what happened next:

> In Harnall Row Kington is waiting for them, with a knife, destined got a bloody purpose, concealed in his pocket. He pushes the brother aside, requests his wife to go with him, she refuses, they wrangle, and the brother leaves them to be in time for his work.
>
> Against her will the woman is, as it were, forced along South Street and the lane at the back of Gosford Street, slowly, stopping occasionally, she opposing passive ill-temper against the increasing torrent of his fierce wrath. An acquaintance at a weaver's shop window observed them while thus – the man gesticulating – the woman so little absorbed in the scene, that

she recognised her acquaintance and nodded and smiled twice.

In fact the peculiarity of this woman appears to have been that she was not capable of receiving any strong impression. Fully aware of her danger, she was yet so little impressed by it that she took no steps to get out of her husband's power, which she might of course have done easily in the public streets of Coventry; and when, as he forced her into Swan Lane, she was sufficiently roused to do something for her protection, she took the tame step of asking a milk boy to send a policeman after them, rather than simply separating herself, during any portion of the walk, from the man, and invoking the aid of passers-by.

They went along Swan Lane, through the fields leading thence to Payne's Lane, and as soon as they got through the posts which lead into the last of those fields, within sight of Payne's Lane, in a much-frequented footpath, and necessarily within hearing of many people who would assuredly be about the place at nine o'clock in the morning, the fearful deed was performed.[59]

The deed referred to was, to use the phrase employed by the journalist, fearful indeed.

Mary Ann Pickard, who knew the Kingtons, was walking through the field adjoining Payne's Lane on her way to work at nearby Jeffrey Wood's Cross when she heard screaming. Looking over the hedge, she saw John Kington with one leg kneeling on the ground, with Elizabeth laying across it as he pulled her down. He had a knife in his hand. As Mary Ann stood there, unable to move, she heard Elizabeth pleaded for forgiveness, but her husband responded, "I've forgiven you enough times already; you might thank your father for it all – if he were here I'd serve him the same."

At that, John Kington took the knife and cut her throat deep to the bone. He then put his hand into the wound, saying he'd take it out.

James Jones, a labourer returning from the shop of a Mr Potter at Jeffrey Wood's Cross, saw a young girl named Elizabeth Ann Elliott in the lane, and as both entered the field which led to Payne's Lane they heard a muffled scream. Reaching the end of a hedge, Jones

59   *Coventry Standard*, 19 November 1859.

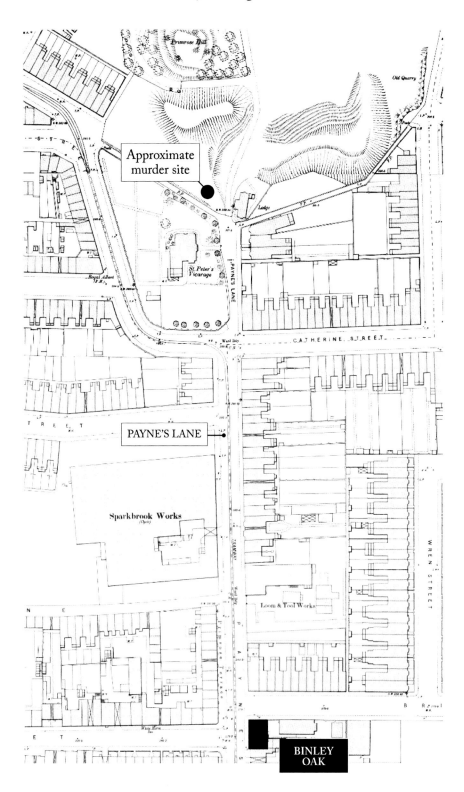

Approximate murder site

PAYNE'S LANE

saw John Kington kneeling on the body of his wife.

> He then jumped up, and his features seemed distorted with
> passion. He held the knife in the air as if going to stab me. He
> seemed to be so overcome with passion that he could not speak.
> His teeth grated and his hand seemed to tremble with passion.
> The sight of the woman so far overcome me that I partially
> dropped on the posts. The little girl Elliott clung to me.

A labourer named James Edmunds was working on a building on
Adelaide Street when he was alerted to the murder; he went to the
field and saw John Kington standing alongside the body of his dead
wife. The murderer told him, matter-of-factly, "I've done; I'd have
cut her head off if I could, but I couldn't, the knife bent." He agreed
to go with Edmunds to the Police station.

On duty at Coventry Police station was Sergeant Salmon –
promoted since his arrest of Susannah Jarvis fifteen years earlier
– who was told that a murder had been committed in a field near
Payne's Lane.

Heading off to the scene, the officer met Kington walking quite
calmly with James Edmunds, heading towards him. They were by
the Pool Meadow. A nearby bell rang out to mark the hour; it was
nine o'clock.

Kington said he'd go quietly, and in response to Sergeant Salmon's
query as to the whereabouts of the knife, said:

> It lies by the side of her. She's dead enough. It is her father's
> fault; if she had went and lived with me last night this would not
> have happened, but I am satisfied now.

Claiming that Elizabeth's last words had been "It's my father's
fault, God bless you, goodbye," Kington told the officer that he
would have also stabbed Samuel Holmes if he'd been close enough
to him.

Salmon told another officer with him, PC Jackson, to find the
body and stay with it until he returned. In the meantime the
sergeant took Kington into custody at the station.

He then made his way to view the body of poor Elizabeth

Kington, which was lying in a field accessed from Payne's Lane, near the Parsonage at the back of Primrose Hill.

The office had sent a constable to the Binley Oak, along the other end of Payne's Lane, and a door was procured – whether a spare or a door dismounted from its hinges is unrecorded. But on arrival at the blood-soaked field, the body was placed upon the make-shift stretcher and conveyed back to the pub along the street – surely under cover to avoid alarming onlookers.

There, local surgeon Mr William Dresser arrived and examined the body. His description of the wounds given to the coroner's inquest at the Binley Oak on the Monday – 14 November – was sobering:

> On the right hand side of the head there was a gash down the cheek, severing the principal arteries of the face. There was another cut which was superficial a little below it; and the main injury was to the throat. The carotid artery was divided, and in fact all the arteries to the spine, and the windpipe was severed. The right hand was also badly cut. It is evident that she resisted considerably. It was possible for her to have spoken after the first cut.

Prior to his summing up, Coroner Poole read over the depositions of the witnesses and in the process cautioned Henry Quinney, the milk boy whom Elizabeth Kington had implored to go to the police, to pay more attention to a plea for help such as that made to him by the deceased should a similar one be forthcoming in the future – as though wives being led to their doom by murderous husbands was a regular occurrence – but praised the actions of Mary Ann Pickard.

The jury returned a verdict of Wilful Murder against Kington; not surprising, seeing as he had already admitted his guilt.

On Saturday, 19 November John Kington was brought up before the magistrates. It was noted that he appeared paler, thinner and more more anxious than at the time of his arrest.

Mr Davis, opening for the prosecution, said he did not intend to relay the gruesome details of the murder – those being related by the witnesses to follow – but assured everyone present that "at the close of the examination it will be plain to your minds that. There

The Binley Oak, Payne's Lane,
where Elizabeth's body was taken and the inquest into her death held
Courtesy www.HistoricCoventry.co.uk

can be no about the prisoner is guilty the crime for which he has to answer."

At one point Kington drew groans and other expressions of disgust when he claimed that Elizabeth had remained loyal to him despite her father's interference, commenting in an indifferent tone,

> She never ran away; not one yard, from the time I took her out of Harnall Lane till I killed her – not one yard.

He then took the opportunity to question the witness James Jones, who had seen Kington kneeling upon Elizabeth's body:

Prisoner: When did you see me first?

Witness: I first saw you on the top of your missus.

You came out of Tew's Lane, did you not?

Yes.

We stood at the top when you were in the centre of the lane – we stood against the stile, didn't we?

I never saw you.

You came up between the gardens and the hedge, and we walked on till we got to the top of the field. Did we walk on, or not?

I never saw you till I came on you after you had killed the woman.

Did you not stand and watch us?

No.

Did she not call you before I touched her?

Certainly not. What a wicked man you are.

What did she say to you when she saw me pull the knife out? Did she not say, "Mr Jones, save me?"

No.

At this point someone in the public gallery laughed, causing Kington to turn round in a savage manner and exclaim "I don't want anyone to laugh at me."

Turning back to Mr Jones, the prisoner asked,

> When she asked you to save her, did you not run away and get through the hedge into Payne's Lane?
>
> Certainly not. I never saw you till I came upon you as I have stated.
>
> It's what I said. You ran away first, and when you came back I had murdered her.

Just as with his vendetta against his father in law Samuel Holmes, it was an attempt to ruin the reputation of James Jones.

After hearing all the evidence Mayor Soden cautioned the prisoner, and asked whether he had anything to say. True to form, Kington replied in a surly manner: "Not 'til my trial."

He was then committed to appear at the next assizes.[60]

As fate would have it, Kington would not have long to await his trial. The Winter Assizes at Warwick opened on Monday 19 December, just a month later, and on the second day the wife murderer had his turn in the dock. His time in the cells seemed to have weakened his attitude; he now appeared compliant, and pleaded Guilty to the crime. When the judge commented that he hoped the plea was not an attempt to create a favourable impression,

60   *Coventry Herald*, 25 November 1859.

Kington replied in a quiet voice that it was no use; he could not plead against his conscience.

Kington then handed the judge a piece of paper, which His Honour took several minutes to read. Despite the prisoner's pleas, he declined to read out the contents in public, telling him:

> I have read it through. It appears to me that it is not advisable that it should be read in public. You know to what I allude.

Minutes later, Mr Justice Williams Put on the black cap, and said:

> Prisoner at the bar, you have been found Guilty on your confession of the murder of your wife. I have read through the dispositions of the witnesses before the coroner and the committing magistrates, and having done so, and finding their evidence inclusive, it is not a matter of surprise or regret to me that you have thought it better to plead Guilty, not in the hopes of obtaining mercy in this world, but from a consciousness that the evidence was overwhelming, and in order to avoid the pain of hearing the details of your crime proved by the witnesses in face of the public.
>
> You have handed in a paper, which I have read, and which I will take care shall be forwarded to the proper quarter. But I am bound to say that there is nothing in it to justify you in hoping that mercy will be extended to you. I have prayed you not to have that paper read in public. It contains imputations on others of the most dreadful kind, and I should regret that the last act of your life should have been to impute to others such a dreadful time as that which you have suggested.
>
> I have no wish to increase your pain, but it is my duty to pass upon you the sentence of the law, and I can hold out to you no hope of mercy, in this world.[61]

What did the note reveal? Was it some scandal attached to Elizabeth Kington? Some commentators on the case wondered whether there had been an incestuous relationship between her and her father, Samuel Holmes – even that he had fathered her illegitimate child born before she met John Kington – which would

61 *Wigton Advertiser*, 24 December 1859.

explain Kington's claim that Holmes was the cause of all their problems. Making a claim of this kind against the man who saw as his nemesis would have been one last attempt at revenge.

Personally, I think that unlikely. It's more probable that Mr Holmes was protective of his daughter, concerned about her welfare – especially given his wife had died five years earlier and he was a former Police officer – and that of his granddaughter, Martha, given John Kington's violent disposition, and one newspaper hinted at this in their coverage of the magistrates' hearing:

> Probably the interference of the wife's father in their quarrels, coupled with the wife's behaviour towards himself, and apparent reliance on her father, gave rise to a suspicion in Kington's morbidly jealous and exacting mind, as to the object of the visits of his wife to her father, a suspicion too horrible to be expressed in print, and in confirmation of which no single circumstance has been adduced before any regular tribunal.[62]

Yet Samuel Holmes felt his reputation had been so stained by the whispered accusations that he felt compelled to apply to the magistrates that they investigate the matter, so as to clear his name. His letter to Justice of the Peace Mr Morris – and the reply – were published in the *Coventry Weekly Times* of 30 November 1859:

> Nov. 20, 1859.
>
> Worshipful Sir, – I trust you will pardon my presumption in writing to you in reference to the late melancholy occurrence, the murder of my daughter, as in connection therewith the most shameful and unfounded charges have been circulated, very injurious to my character.
>
> One of the newspaper reports of the incidents of the murder is full of falsehoods, to pander to the morbid tastes of the public. These false reports are of so horrible a nature that I earnestly hope you will request your Brother Visiting Justices, with yourself, to give me and my witnesses an opportunity of coming before you, that you may hear them in refutation of the vile and groundless charges made against me. I feel it is due to myself and the character of my other children in after life, that the whole

62 *Coventry Standard*, 19 November 1859.

affair should be investigated, when I have no fear of appearing before you at the close of the enquiry exonerated and innocent of these base imputations.

If you, gentlemen, will kindly grant me this, and direct Mr Mann, the Governor of the Gaol, to give me notice when you will assemble, I shall be extremely obliged, in order that the public mind may be disabused and set right upon this very painful affair.

I have the honour to be your obedient, humble servant,
SAMUEL HOLMES.

The reply of Mr Morris JP, dated 25 November, then appeared:

Sir, – The visiting Magistrates, before whom I laid your letter addressed to me on the 20th inst., have requested me to inform you they cannot interfere in the matter in question. I therefore advise you to obtain from Mr Twist a copy of the application of your late daughter to the Magistrates for a summons for the appearance of the reputed father of the child, which must greatly relieve you from the unpleasant rumours now in circulation.

The *Times* then revealed that the document alluded to by Mr Morris – a letter from Elizabeth naming the father of her illegitimate child – had indeed been obtained from the magistrates, and was now in the possession of the recently retired Inspector John Vice of the Coventry City Police. He was retaining it, said the *Times*, "to produce it in a Superior Court when required. Mr Vice will give every information upon the subject, being acquainted with all the circumstances of the case."

With the required information at his fingertips should he need it, Samuel Holmes was satisfied.

His son-in-law, the evil John Kington, was hanged on a scaffold in front of Warwick Gaol on Friday, 30 December 1859.[63] His body was buried within the prison boundary.[64]

*

---

63   *North & South Shields Gazette*, 5 January 1860.
64   Ledger of Persons Tried at Warwick Assizes, December 1859.

Samuel Holmes took the infant Martha, now orphaned following the murder of her mother and execution of her father, into his home at Court 12, House 8, Far Gosford Street. With Elizabeth dead, his six other children – ranging from twenty-one year old Martha to ten year old James – remained living at home.[65] It's not hard to see what a tight-knit unit the Holmes family were, and why Samuel was so keen to look out for his eldest daughter's welfare.

Baby Martha was baptised at St Michael's on 4 January 1860, a week after her father's execution.[66] Tragically, her uncle Walter – who had attempted to protect his sister from John Kington – died in 1863, aged just twenty-two.[67]

Sadly, the 1871 Census shows that Martha had been sent to the Asylum for Poor Orphan Girls at Bristol, where she is recorded as one of fifty inmate pupils under the tutelage of Miss Hannah Walham.

The same census reveals the reason why; her grandfather Samuel Holmes was residing at the Coventry Union Workhouse, a pauper inmate. He died there months later, on 13 October 1871, and was buried in an unmarked pauper's grave two days later.[68] He was just fifty-five years old.

Martha is next recorded in official documents when she married Henry Mear, a decorator, at south London, on 29 May 1880. She was at this time twenty-two years old, Mr Mear a fifty year old widower.[69]

The couple settled at Battersea, and two daughters joined them: Emily (1881-1964) and Rosa (1884-1961). Despite their age difference, Henry and Martha spent many happy years together, before Henry passed away in May 1909, just four days short of their twenty-eighth wedding anniversary.[70]

Two years later, in the 1911 Census, Martha is recorded as living

65 1861 Census.
66 Baptism record of Martha Elizabeth Kington.
67 Death registers.
68 *Coventry Standard*, 13 October 1871; Burial records.
69 Marriage certificate of Henry Mear and Martha Kington.
70 Probate record of Henry Mear, 20 May 1909.

with daughter Emily, her husband Reginald and their son Clifford at Carshalton in Surrey.

She died in October 1922, at the age of sixty-four, and was buried at Sutton Cemetery.[71]

71   UK, Burial and Cremation Index, 1838–2014: Martha Elizabeth Mear, 31 October 1922.

DECEMBER 1859

BRIDGET BUTLER

Sitting on Greyfriars Lane since 1509, Ford's Hospital[72] has long provided a safe haven for the elderly of Coventry, originally acting as an almshouse.

But in the early hours of 28 November 1859 it was the silent observer to a horrific event which place in the courtyard of the house adjoining its left side; an incident as far removed from William Ford's benevolent intention of providing sanctuary as can be imagined.

It was still dark when fifty-eight year old William Muddiman woke and heard a child's cries. Getting out of bed, he went down the stairs of Mr Brannan's lodging house and to the back door, where he heard another cry coming from Court No. 5, which served a number of houses on Greyfriars Lane. Peering into the gloom, Muddiman was unable to see the cause of the noises so went back to bed.

But now awake, a quarter of an hour later the old man was up again and fetched a light before going into the yard to visit the privy.

---

72   More properly known as Grey Friars Hospital, it was founded using an endowment by merchant William Ford to provide accommodation for six elderly people. The endowment was extended in the years following Ford's death and by 1846 it was serving forty women. Ford's Hospital was hit during enemy action on 14 October 1940, with the warden, a nurse and six residents being killed. It was restored with original timbers between 1951 and 1953.

The timber-beamed Ford's Hospital, centre,
with the lodging house run by Mr Brannan on the left
Courtesy www.HistoricCoventry.co.uk

Now, the cries seemed muffled. They seemed to be coming from the direction of the 'dust hole', where the ashes from the fireplaces belonging to each of the houses which backed on to the court were dumped.

Clearing away the cold ashes from the small pit with his bare hands, Muddiman touched what he thought was a human arm. He reached in and took hold of a naked baby, buried more than a foot beneath the ash and soot. Shocked, he quickly the newborn back into the light and warmth of Brannan's.

There, Mrs Margaret Hughes – who lodged next door at Mrs Donnelly's – had her own story to tell. She too had been woken by the cries, and minutes before Mr Muddiman went into the court had also searched the yard. She later told the magistrates:

> I heard a smothered noise, but I could not say that it was caused by a child. I went and borrowed a candle from Brannan, searched the privy, and looked on the dust hole, but did not look beneath the ashes. I could not find anything, and returned to my lodgings. Directly afterwards I heard that the child had been found. I went into Brannan's and saw the child. It was so completely covered with ashes that it was hard to tell what it was.

Mrs Hughes warmed the infant by the fire, and gave it a good wash. It took three bowls of clean water to remove all the ash and soot from the little body, which was now thankfully gaining some colour. It was a newborn girl, just minutes old.

Three women then entered the room; Bridget Donnelly, the owner of the house next door, her niece Margaret, and a young Irishwoman. Mrs Hughes turned to the latter, who had arrived in Coventry just weeks earlier calling herself Bridget Butler, and told her to sit by the fire and take her child. When Miss Butler said that the baby wasn't hers, she was told that the Police and a doctor were on their way, and it would be better if the child was on her lap when they arrived than Mrs Hughes'.

Butler took the baby, and Mrs Hughes went upstairs to get dressed.

Dr Edward Bicknell, surgeon attached to the Coventry Union Workhouse, arrived and went upstairs with Bridget Butler and Mrs

Brannan to a bedroom, where he examined the young Irishwoman. Soon after, the doctor went back downstairs and told PC McDermot,[73] who had arrived in his absence, that he was convinced Miss Butler had given birth within a few hours.[74] He recommended that both mother and child be taken to the Workhouse, which the officer did by cab, delivering them into the care of the Matron of the Infirmary.

The following morning PC McDermot returned to the facility and fetched Miss Butler, taking her to the Police Office where she was charged with attempted child murder. She no longer denied being the child's mother; her only response was that she was not in her right mind at the time. The reason for her anxiety would soon become apparent.

It was believed that the child's life had been saved by the fact that some paper and old bonnets had been earlier cast into the ash pit, these bulkier items preventing the ashes from suffocating her.[75]

*

Bridget Butler had arrived at the house of Mrs Donnelly in the middle of October 1859. She was given work washing the clothes and bed linen of the residents of the various houses in the court, and all commented on the fact she was in the family way; a claim she strenuously denied. She had given her name as Bridget Butler, although it was generally understood that she was really Bridget Buckney or Buckley. Some newspapers reported her alias as Margaret Welch or Welsh.

Whatever her real name, the reason for her sudden appearance in Coventry was soon revealed.

Heavily pregnant she may have been, but her husband – a marine

---

73 PC John McDermot had served previously with the Birmingham Police, and was transferred to the Coventry City Police after more than a dozen years' service. Two years after the incident with Bridget Butler he and wife Martha took in Oliver Style's sister Caroline as an apprentice, only for her to rob them. See *The Watchmaker's Revenge* by Adam Wood.
74 *Coventry Herald* and Observer, 16 December 1859.
75 *Coventry Times*, 14 December 1859.

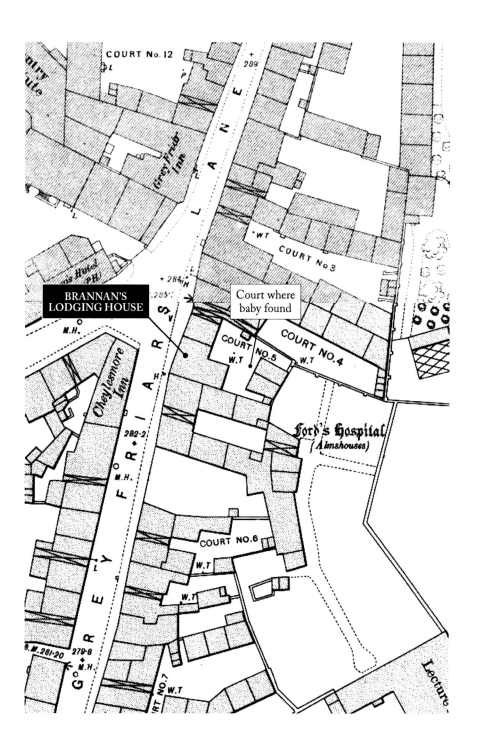

store dealer at Bilston, near Wolverhampton – had been convicted of receiving stolen goods three years earlier and was languishing in prison. His sentence was due to expire in March 1860, and his surprise at being greeted on his return home by his wife with a babe in arms might well be imagined.[76] A reporter from the *Coventry Standard* hinted that Mr Buckley might not have been totally taken aback by the actions of his thirty-three year old wife:

> Her husband's last letter expressed apprehension that all was not right, as he could not understand her removed to Coventry, and conveyed a hope that he should find the home as he left it on his return. In reply he received an assurance that there would be the home to go to, but that his wife had come temporarily to Coventry in consequence of being unable to obtain work.[77]

As her time grew close, Butler slept in the same bed as Mrs Donnelly for three nights. In the small hours of 28 November she woke her landlady by getting out of bed and going downstairs. When she returned half an hour later she lay on the bed, fully clothed, until Mrs Donnelly persuaded her to get under the covers. After a short sleep the two women got up, and between seven and eight o'clock were working together, washing clothes.

But very soon afterwards the landlady's little boy walked in and said a baby had been found. When Mrs Donnolly commented that, as the infant was still alive, the mother must still be nearby, Bridget Butler rather unnervingly replied "That baby's mother will never be found."[78]

*

The young Irishwoman had very little time to wait for her turn in the dock. She appeared at the Warwickshire Winter Assizes, which commenced on Thursday, 15 December at the Shire Hall in Warwick. She was the next defendant to appear after John Kington,

---

76   *Coventry Herald* and Observer, 2 December 1859.
77   *Coventry Standard*, 3 December 1859.
78   *Coventry Herald* and Observer, 16 December 1859.

whose despicable crime was related above.

There was no doubt as to her guilt, and the jury swiftly returned a verdict that effect. On hearing their prounouncement, the prisoner fainted in the dock and was carried out of court. She was returned on the Monday morning to receive the sentence; three years' imprisonment.[79]

Far worse than an episode of fainting was to come for Bridget Butler. Before the trial she had shown little interest in her daughter, and had reportedly acted cruelly towards her. Since the Guilty verdict she had become unhinged, and was taken to Hatton Asylum as a criminal lunatic. As a result, on 12 December the baby was taken from her,[80] having previously been cared for at the Coventry Union Workhouse. Now, it was under the protection of Mrs Mann, who was the wife of Coventry Gaol's Governor George Mann.

Three days later – on 15 December 1859, the day the Warwickshire Assizes opened – the infant was taken to St Michael's and baptised. She had been named by her mother while at the workhouse,[81] and it was as Rose Ann Butler that she was baptised. Her mother's abode was given as the County Gaol, and the ceremony was carried out by Rev Saunders, Chaplain of the prison.[82]

Intriguingly, the baptismal register lists the father as one Thomas O'Neil, probably on information given by Bridget herself. Assuming the affair took place in Bilston, her place of residence before her flight to Coventry, a scan of local records shows just one possible candidate: Thomas O'Neil, at the time of the tryst a married twenty-nine year old Irishman.[83]

On 20 December, following her mother's conviction, Rose Anne was handed over to Mrs Esther Young, matron of Coventry Gaol, who would look after the infant for the next eight months. In August 1860 she was transferred to Warwick Union Workhouse,

---

79   *Leamington Advertiser*, 22 December 1859.
80   *Coventry Herald*, 30 November 1860; *Leamington Spa Courier*, 1 December 1860.
81   *Coventry Herald*, 30 November 1860.
82   Baptismal record of Rose Ann Butler.
83   1861 and 1871 census returns.

under the care of master Joseph Hilton. Bridget Butler was taken from Hatton on just one occasion to visit her daughter. It was reported that, although still unsound of mind, she did recognise the infant.

At the end of November 1860 Coventry Assistant Overseer Mr Margetts applied to the court that Rose Ann Butler be adjudged as having a settlement to St Nicholas Parish, Coventry. This was granted, and the child came under the care of the authorities.[84]

*

This would have been perhaps the happiest ending for this story. However, there was a sad postscript.

On 1 August 1862, on reporting on events at the Magistrates' Court, the *Coventry Standard* carried the following:

ROW AT THE WORKHOUSE

Sarah Dunn, an inmate of the Workhouse, was charged, on the information of Mr Bird, master of the Workhouse, with assaulting another woman named Bridget Butler. Mr Harris said he was in his office on Saturday, and, hearing a great disturbance, went to see what was the cause of it. He found that it arose in the following circumstances:

A woman named Bridget Butler, some time ago, was sentenced to penal servitude for placing her newborn child in a dust-hole in Greyfriars Lane, with intent to murder it, but the child was found alive and recovered. The woman had returned from penal servitude and took the child from the Workhouse, but it had fallen ill. She had taken it back to the house, where it died.

It seemed that some of the women at the Workhouse fancied that the woman's conduct had caused the death of the infant, and therefore they took an opportunity of putting her under the pump. The only one he could identify was the defendant.

On the woman giving a promise not to offend again, the case was not pressed.[85]

84 *Leamington Spa Courier*, 1 December 1860.
85 *Coventry Standard*, 1 August 1862.

The reaction of Sarah Dunn and her companions at the Workhouse can be easily understood; young Rose Ann Buckley, now approaching three years old, would have received care and nourishment at the facility, away from the mother who had seemingly never displayed any affection. But just a few short months of the woman's release from prison, her daughter was dead. Had she truly recovered from the insanity which had caused her temporary removal to Hatton Asylum?

There is no record of the wretched Bridget Buckley after this incident. In all probability she adopted another name – as she had with Margaret Welsh and Bridget Butler – and disappeared into the mists of time.

WILLIAM BEAMISH

The *Black Kalendar* contains many stories of wrongdoing, but it has to be said that none of the people involved were criminal masterminds; they had been driven by greed, desperation, mental illness or, as in the following case, by lust.

William Beamish was to all intents and purposes a decent man. He had been the first child born to weaver David and his wife Susannah in 1826, and was baptised at St Michael's on 11 September that year.[86] Both his parents were just twenty years old.[87]

By the time of the 1841 Census the family were living on Spon Street. William was now fifteen, and was working like his parents as a ribbon weaver. He had been joined by two sisters, Emma and Harriett, and brothers Aaron and Daniel.

On 11 August 1849 William was back at St Michael's, this time for his wedding to Betsey Stokes. She was the same age, having been born to William and Millicina, weavers of Freeth Street. Betsey had been baptised at St Michael's on 13 March 1826, just six months before her future husband.[88]

They didn't waste any time starting a family following the marriage. A son, William Jr, was born late in 1850; the census taken in March the following year records the infant as just five months old. The family were living on Albion Street at this time,

---

86 Baptismal record of William Beamish.
87 Ages taken from 1841 Census.
88 Marriage register; Baptismal record of Betsey Stokes.

with William Beamish working as a power loom weaver and Betsey a silk winder.[89]

Tragically, a period of sadness lay ahead. Over the next five years William and Betsey lost three children at a tender age; Alfred (1851-1853), Harriet (1854-1855) and Josiah (born and died in 1856).[90]

So when another daughter, Lizzie, was born on 2 November 1857,[91] the couple must have anticipated the worst; thankfully, the girl survived and a sister, Emily, was born towards the end of 1859.[92]

By the time of the 1861 Census, taken on 7 April, the Beamish family were well settled at 28 Spencer Street, having been there for much of the previous decade.[93] They enjoyed a respectable position in society, with William, now thirty-four, working as a silk weaver. Betsey was carrying out the same work, and children William Jr (known as 'Willie', aged nine), Lizzie[94] (three) and Emily (one) were thriving.[95]

William Beamish was by all accounts well liked by everyone. Charles Read, a watchmaker who had known him for fifteen years and who would later become entangled in the web of deceit, commented that he was an honest and industrious young man.

As if to underline this point, Beamish had for eighteen months also taught at the Sunday School attached to the Well Street Chapel at which the family worshipped. The minister, Rev Phillip Barker,

---

89 1851 Census. Albion Street was part of the maze of streets surrounding the Butts and Queen's Road. It was demolished to make way for the Coventry Ring Road in the 1960s.

90 Birth and Death registers.

91 Date of birth from 1939 Register of England and Wales.

92 Birth register.

93 Inquest testimony of Charlotte Wright, who said she had lived on Spencer Street near the Beamishes for seven years, and they had already been at No. 28 when she moved next door.

94 The name is spelt in different ways across newspaper and census returns, sometimes as Lizzy. I have taken the spelling from the 1911 Census return, which was written down by her husband George Munton – who would surely know how his wife's name was spelt.

95 1861 Census.

said that he had an excellent character.[96]

William Beamish had reached a good stage in his life. In addition to gaining the respect of the community, work was going well. Rather that working solely at home, he also worked in a factory at Hillfields,[97] owned by James Hart,[98] where one of his workers was a young lady named Emma Statham.

And that's where his problems began.

*

Emma Statham had been born to Thomas and Sarah, a hardworking sawyer and his wife, at the end of 1837. She was baptised at Holy Trinity on 13 February 1838, joining elder sister Jane. A brother, Tom, and two more girls – Selina and Sarah Ann – joined the growing Statham clan.

By the time she began working at Mr Hart's factory, Emma was twenty-three and unmarried. William Beamish was thirty-five and very much married. Still, that didn't deter him from starting an affair.

Mrs Sarah Turner, who lived opposite the Beamish house on Spencer Street, later told the inquest that she had known William Beamish for eight or nine years, and he had always been very kind and affectionate toward this wife Betsey, until around eighteen months ago when he became acquainted with Emma Statham.

Mrs Turner had first seen the lovers together the summer before last, when they were sitting on the grass among the trees near the Stivichall Arms, by the common. He had his arm around her waist, and she had her hand in his.

One afternoon a few weeks later Mrs Turner happened to go into the Shepherd and Shepherdess pub on the Keresley Road, and sat

---

96   *Coventry Times*, 4 September 1861.
97   *Salisbury and Winchester Journal*, 14 September 1861.
98   *Coventry Standard*, 30 August 1861. A news item in the *Coventry Times* of 25 May 1859 about a dispute between Mr Hart and his workers at the factory reveal not only his forename, but also that the factory was situated on West Orchard.

The Shepherd and Shepherdess
Courtesy www.HistoricCoventry.co.uk

in the bar to drink a half pint of ale. As she sipped her drink, she glanced through door leading into the parlour and saw William Beamish and Emma Statham sitting together in the other room, kissing and holding hands. Mrs Turner left without saying anything.

She appears to have seen the not-so-secretive couple several times over the coming months, even in his own workshop. On this occasion Mrs Turner could not help but see all; her attic bedroom overlooked Beamish's workshop, the large windows of which – installed to permit light for weaving work – now had a different use.

Sarah Turner told Betsey Beamish what she'd seen, receiving the reply that the wronged wife "could never go anywhere without being told of his goings-on."

William was a man with just one thing on his mind.

*

On the morning of 14 August 1861 Mrs Charlotte Wright, who

lived next door to the Beamish family, was told by her daughter that Betsey, her son Willie and daughter Emily were all sick. As if by way of confirmation, soon afterwards she heard Betsey vomiting in her kitchen next door. She went round and asked if she had taken anything which disagreed with her, to which Betsey replied:

> Oh, no; we have only had some coffee, and the children have had some bread and dripping and some bread and treacle and, to tell you the truth, I was eating a bit of dry bread myself.

Agreeing that there was nothing in that simple meal which should have caused sickness, Mrs Wright returned to her house but soon heard Betsey vomiting again. Mr Beamish was out of the house, having left for his workshop without partaking of breakfast.

Later that evening, around dinner time, Mrs Wright saw Betsey once more, and remarked that she looked ill. The stricken woman replied, "I feel very ill indeed."

Around eleven o'clock on the following morning Dr Goate was called to the house, and examined Betsey Beamish. She complained of a pain in her chest and throat, and that she had bowel problems. The doctor noted that the inside of her mouth was very much damaged, which had probably been caused by her continued vomiting.[99]

He was told that little Emily was also ill, with the same complaint of a sore mouth and extreme diarrhoea, but on visiting the infant's bedroom found her asleep and did not wake her, as she seemed comfortable.

Dr Goate was a little surprised, therefore, when William Beamish arrived at his office the next morning asking for a death certificate, as his daughter had passed away in the night. The medical man said the death had been very sudden, but based upon the description given by Beamish duly supplied a death certificate listing the cause as 'diarrhoea'.[100]

The next morning, around nine o'clock, William Beamish and

99 *Coventry Weekly Times*, 28 August 1861.
100 *Coventry Standard*, 7 September 1861.

Emma Statham were back in his workshop, up to their tricks. Sarah Turner, watching from her attic window, saw him kiss her and put his hand up her petticoats.[101] It seemed that not even the death of his child and ongoing ill-health of his wife could stop the former Sunday school teacher from pursuing his amorous intentions.

Little Emma was buried at the London Road Cemetery two days later, on Sunday, 18 August. Afterwards, Betsey's sister Emily – married to weaver John Harrow and living on East Street – went back to the Beamishes' house. There, Betsey went into the outside privy and asked Emily to look into her mouth, enquiring whether it looked the same as Emily's had when she'd contracted cholera.

Emily looked into her mouth and noted that the tongue was very red and dry. Before going into the house Betsey told her sister that she needed to urinate, but it burned when she did so. Eventually, Emily and William helped her indoors and into bed. There, she had a cup of tea and some arrowroot, brought to her by Emma Statham, and was immediately sick.[102]

Dr Goate was called back to the house on the Monday, and noted that while Betsey seemed on the whole better, her lips and mouth looked the same as they had on the Friday. Then, as in the case with little Emily, the following morning William Beamish turned on the doctor's doorstep asking for a death certificate, as Betsey had passed away in the night. Dr Goate was startled and refused, saying that a post mortem was required. Beamish made no comment, but the good doctor noted that he appeared agitated.[103]

A brief but sorrowful announcement was placed in the Deaths column of the *Coventry Standard*, appearing on Friday, 23 August:

> On the 15th inst., aged 1 year, Emily; and on the 20th inst., aged 33 years, Betsy, daughter and wife of William Beamish, of Spencer Street.

That afternoon William Beamish told Jane Stokes, Betsey's sister

101 *Coventry Weekly Times*, 4 September 1861.
102 *Coventry Herald*, 30 August 1861.
103 *Coventry Weekly Times*, 28 August 1861.

who had attended her during her short illness, that he would like to check the pockets of his wife's dresses to see what was in them – a strange request, but Jane agreed and led him upstairs to the back room where her sister kept her clothes. She picked up the dress that Betsey had been wearing on the day she had first been taken ill, and Beamish put his hand in the pocket and took out a purse, which he opened. Inside he found a note.

Almost immediately Beamish exclaimed, "Oh, Jane"– she was sure he didn't have time to read the note's contents – and handed it to her. She put it into her pocket and followed him downstairs, for William Beamish "seemed very much agitated, raved and ran about like a madman."

Jane would later hand the note to Inspector Payne. It read as follows; spelling and punctuation (or lack of it) retained:

> For Jane Stokes
>
> Dr Sister – if anything happns to me doo not let them blame any one but god forgive me I did not know what I was doing but the thought of lossing my home and to see how the poor lad was fretin to know wat to do for the moment drove me mad for to lose my home I could not bare the disgrace after living respectful so long and do not tel him if you elp it for it will drive him mad Jane see to the little one for he is so fond of Lizzy God bles and comfort my poor lad
>
> Betsy Beamish 14th Aug.

This was strange, as Jane Stokes would later say that she have never seen or known her sister to write. As far as she knew she had not been to school, but could read.[104]

William Beamish, on the other hand, could write.

Inspector Frederick Payne, on receiving the note, discovered that it was a sheet of paper torn from an old memorandum book, which he found in a cupboard in the front room of Beamish's house.

He went in search of the supposed bereaved husband, and found him on Raglan Street at eleven o'clock that night. Searching him, Inspector Payne found a packet of poison in the breast pocket of

---

104 *Coventry Herald*, 30 August 1861.

his coat.

William Beamish was arrested on suspicion of murder.

*

The Gloucester Arms,
where the inquest took place
Courtesy www.HistoricCoventry.co.uk

When the post mortem revealed the presence of poison in Betsey Beamish's system, her daughter Emily was exhumed. This time, there was little doubt that death had been caused by arsenical poisoning, and the coroner's jury sitting at the Gloucester Arms on Stoney Stanton Road heard evidence as to William Beamish's illicit affair with Emma Statham, and also that he had visited a number of chemists around Coventry asking for arsenic saying it was to treat an infestation of rats. They wasted no time in returning a verdict of Wilful Murder.[105]

Following suit, Coventry's magistrates quickly committed William Beamish to trial at the forthcoming Winter Assizes at Warwick.

THE CONVICTION OF WILLIAM BEAMISH.

This case, which has excited more interest in this city than any case within the memory of the oldest inhabitant, has terminated fatally to the prisoner. Throughout the whole of yesterday [17 December] the excitement was intense – almost painful. It appears that the prisoner confidently anticipated that the verdict

105 *Coventry Weekly Times*, 28 August 1861.

would be in his favour. Many people entertained the same opinion, thinking that there was an important link wanting in the chain of evidence to substantiate the charge.

The remarks of the Judge in his charge to the Grand Jury very much favoured this opinion, and made even those who had little doubt of a conviction previously begin to think that it might even turn out to the prisoner's advantage. His friends spared neither trouble nor expense to obtain for him eminent counsel, and up to the time of the summing up of the learned Judge there was a faint hope that the trial might end in a verdict of acquittal. The summing up was very thorough, and decided unfavourable to the prisoner.

As the trial approached the termination, the suspense was almost intolerable; and when the Foreman of the Jury entered into Court, after an absence of about a quarter of an hour, the eyes of the prisoner were riveted upon him. Another moment, and the fatal word 'Guilty' sealed his fate.[106]

The verdict appeared to take Beamish completely by surprise; when the Foreman of the jury made his pronouncement, the prisoner had to clutch the rail in front of the dock to prevent himself from falling, and it was only with the aid of two wardens that he was able to leave the dock.[107]

William Beamish had not long to idle in the Warwick cells. The date of his execution was set for Monday, 30 December,[108] and he was to be hanged alongside John Thompson, who had cut the throat of his 'partner' of three months, Ann Walker, at a brothel in Birmingham in September.[109] Both condemned men seemed resigned to their fate; Thompson appeared completely indifferent, while Beamish retreated to his religious teachings.[110]

He was allowed a visit from his family, and the final embrace between father and his children was moving. Beamish was visibly upset that little Lizzie, four years old, did not at first recognise him

---

106 *Coventry Weekly Times*, 18 December 1861.
107 *Coventry Herald*, 1 November 1861.
108 *Berkshire Chronicle*, 28 December 1861.
109 *Wigan Observer and District Advertiser*, 5 October 1861.
110 *Berkshire Chronicle*, 28 December 1861.

due to the prison uniform he was made to wear.

When the day came, the double hanging unsurprisingly drew a large crowd, who no doubt looked forward to a day of 'entertainment'. The following newspaper report gives a striking insight into the mindset of an era where public executions were treated as a spectacle:

> From a very early hour in the morning people had been rapidly coming into Warwick from the country villages around, in order that they might secure a good place from which to view the awful spectacle of the execution; and before five o'clock not a few persons had come by the road from Birmingham and Coventry, and had taken up their position in front of the prison, where a strong detachment of the county police was stationed to preserve order.
>
> By the early trains from Birmingham, Coventry and Leamington the number of passengers who arrived was very great. Most of them at once proceeded straight to the prison, where they took their places, and waited in the nipping cold with the greatest of patience of several hours, rather than lose the opportunity of experiencing the momentary but terrible 'sensation' that was to follow.
>
> Amongst all these early appearances there was a striking similarity of appearance; they were nearly all short, thick-set, bull-necked, full-lipped men – men who had a notable affinity to the bull-dog, and who are seldom seen in great number together unless it be at a ratting match, a prize-fight, or an execution.
>
> By about eight o'clock a number of cart-loads of people, including many women who were respectably dressed, but whose presence in such a scene was a sufficient proof as to their character, came in from Coventry, and were arranged in the little lane nearly parallel with the main road, where each formed the standing place of an excited crowd. From this time the crowd in front of the gaol continued to increase, and by the time fixed for the execution about four thousand persons were present.
>
> Every place which commanded a view of the scaffold was occupied; men were standing on the brick kilns near; sitting on hovels, the roofs of which threatened to give way, and thus add a new tragical element to the occasion; lining the banks of the canal, from which a good view could be obtained; and were standing on the slightly elevated ground beyond.

Exterior of Warwick Gaol

The number of women in the crowd had been rapidly increased, and they now formed nearly one-third of the whole; and a large number of children even had made their appearance.

There was very little of that trading under the gallows which is often found at such scene, not were there any of the portable rifle galleries, or of the baked potato men who are usually seen at an execution.

By ten o'clock the crowd had begun to be impatient, and in order to while away the time they swayed about in long waves, and occasionally hoisted one of their number on the heads of the rest, and passed him to the front and back as the whim seized them.

The platform of the scaffold was erected on Saturday afternoon, but it was not until three o'clock on Monday morning that men were seen upon it with lights burning dimly through the thick mist, rendering it complete by the addition of the crossbeam. From the outside of the prison only the upper portions of the scaffold could be seen, all below the floor being hid behind the intervening portion of the building. Depending from the crossbeam were two sets of coupling links, which were about a yard apart, and from each of these depended a rope, at the end of which was the fatal noose. The ropes were both old ones, and

Interior of Warwick Gaol

had both been used before for the purpose for which they were now about so soon to be put.[111]

William Beamish and John Thompson rose around seven o'clock and ate a final breakfast. Prison Chaplain Rev Carles performed a Divine service, then all the prisoners – around two hundred souls – sang psalms, the singing voice of Beamish being noted particularly as firm and clear.

Beamish was then allowed private consultation with Rev Barker from Coventry, to whom he made a full confession of his guilt in murdering his wife, but claimed the death of his little daughter was accidental.

The two condemned men were then handed over to the Under-Sheriff, and executioner George Smith of Dudley began his grim work, pinioning both prisoners.

> At about twelve minutes past ten o'clock one of the turnkeys appeared on the scaffold, immediately followed by Thompson and the executioner. Thomson walked firmly up to his place

111 *Coventry Standard*, 4 January 1862.

under the farthest noose from the steps leading to the scaffold, and appeared to be very little concerned about his fate. There was a curious red flush upon his countenance as he crossed the scaffold. No sooner had he taken his place than the white cap was drawn over his face by Smith, who then swiftly adjusted the noose around his neck. Beamish then ascended the steps to the scaffold with a firm and almost jaunty tread, and the white cap was at once drawn over his face and the noose adjusted. Both the unhappy men wore the prison uniform.

The hangman and the turnkeys then rapidly shook hands with both the prisoners, and immediately Smith disappeared from the scaffold, the bolt was drawn, the floor beneath the feet of the condemned gave way, and they were left suspended by the neck.

Everything had been done so suddenly that the crowd had scarcely comprehended what was to be done before a convulsive shudder passed through it at the sharp clanging sound that told all was over.

No sooner had the drop fallen than there was a peculiar convulsive shudder, and the two twisted round facing each other. After a few muscular contortions Thomson hung a dead mass of clothes and body – for him all was over in this world. It would seen that in consequence of Beamish being a much lighter man than Thompson his neck was not at once dislocated by the fall, and there was a strange tremor of the limbs and body for nearly half a minute.

The moment there was nothing more than two dead bodies suspended on the gallows the crowd began to disperse, and men and women were rushing here and there crying for sale 'The Sorrowful Lamentation of John Thompson, 'The Lamentation of William Beamish', and 'The Trial, Sentence and Awful Execution of John Thompson and William Beamish.'

After the execution it was reported that during his time in prison awaiting his fate William Beamish happened upon another inmate, who had been one of his pupils at the Well Street Chapel Sunday School. Conversation was had as to the dangers of falling off the righteous path.[112]

112 *Coventry Standard*, 4 January 1862.

A similar topic – albeit more to the root of William Beamish's woes – was the subject matter of the Rev Pope's sermon delivered at the Spencer Street Congregational Chapel in Leamington Spa on Sunday 5 January:

> What have we here – a wife murdered by her husband, a child murdered by its father, and what was the cause? Lust. The instigation of lust and impurity did it all. My dear friends, there is no tyrant so exactly; there is no tyrant so gloating; there is no tyrant so insatiable; there is no tyrant so remorseless, as lust. It speaks like this to a young man: For my sake I require thee, young man, to give up they reputation. The young man obeys; his fair reputation vanishes. Then she says – I require thee to steal, and for the sake of lust he becomes a thief. Then she says – I require thee to break thy father and they mother's hearts with grief. He consents. He brings down his parents' grey hairs with sorrow to the grave. Then she still says – I require thee to sacrifice health for my sake, and the young man obeys. He becomes a shadow and a walking skeleton. She said to William Beamish – I require thee to go and purchase poison; I require thee to administer this poison to they wife and to become a murderer, all for the sake of lust… By the gallows of William Beamish, young man, "beware of the strange woman".[113]

Wise words indeed.

Inspired, Ebenezer Price delivered a similar sermon at the Lord Street Sunday School in Chapelfields a week later, titled 'A Voice from the Dungeon'. Heavy reference was made to the actions of William Beamish.[114]

*

The two surviving Beamish children struggled to continue their lives. By the time of the 1871 Census William Jr, then twenty, was living with his uncle Josiah Stokes at the Rainbow inn on Cook Street. Months later he married Emma Bree at Holy Trinity, and

113 *Coventry Times*, 8 January 1862.
114 *Coventry Times*, 8 January 1862.

the couple welcomed daughter Alice and a son, perhaps surprisingly named William, by the time they had moved to Leicestershire. The 1881 Census records them at Blaby, with thirty year old William running a grocery store and, interestingly, serving as the local Methodist preacher. More children were born to the couple; Lilly, Lizzie and Nellie all arrived by 1897.

William Beamish Jr – 'Willie' – lived to a grand old age. He is recorded in the 1939 Register as a retired draper, living at Central Road, Leicester, with his married daughter Nellie. He eventually passed away in the spring of 1946, aged ninety-five.[115]

Lizzy Beamish, mentioned with such affection in the forged suicide letter, also enjoyed a happy life, despite an apparent difficult start; in 1871 she was at the Freeman's Orphan School on Swanswell Terrace, one of seventeen girls receiving an education from teacher Alice Holland.[116]

Ten years later, at the age of twenty-three, she married George Munton,[117] and the couple are recorded in the 1881 Census taken a couple of months later as residing at Hastings Terrace in Birmingham. George was a year younger than his wife, and earning a living as a printer's compositor.

They remained in Birmingham and would have seven children, four of whom survived into adulthood – sons George Jr, Frederick, Harold and William.

By 1901 George Sr was operating his own printing business at home, which at that time was on Hey Hill. The business was still thriving in 1911, although the family had relocated to Wheeler Street. Lizzy was proudly assisting her husband.[118]

But by the time of the 1939 Register age had caught up with them; the couple were living with their son George Jr and his wife Elizabeth, and George Sr is recorded as being 'incapacitated'. He was at this time eighty one, and his wife eighty two. George passed

115 Death Register.
116 1871 Census.
117 Marriage Index.
118 Census returns.

away the following year, and Lizzie – 'little Lizzie – followed on 29 August 1944.[119]

Emma Statham, the unwitting cause of two deaths and the hanging of her lover – she might have been drawn into an illicit liaison with the older man, but surely didn't intend for his wife and young child to die – soon moved on.

It was probably a wise thing; six months after the execution her notoriety saw her name mentioned in a case involving two married women, Mary Norbury and Caroline Fletcher, in which the latter accused Mrs Norbury – who happened to be her mother – of enticing Mr Fletcher to leave the family home. Coventry magistrates heard that Mrs Fletcher had threatened Mrs Norbury, saying she would be "a second Emma Statham to her."[120]

But the real Emma was already making plans to leave Coventry behind. Barely a year after William Beamish was hanged at Warwick, she married Thomas Richardson at Nantwich, Cheshire. He was a locomotive engine fitter, and his work took him all over the country.[121]

It was no doubt appealing to leave Coventry, although the 1871 Census records the married Emma at the home of her parents on Albert Street, Coventry, with her daughter Emily, who had been born in 1867. As an indication of her father's work, the little girl had been born in New Cross, south east London.

1881 saw the Richardsons finally settled, at West Street in Monks Coppenhall, Crewe, where Emma and Thomas had married eighteen years earlier. In addition to daughter Emily, the family also comprised Sarah, Thomas and Minnie, who had been born just a month before the enumerator knocked on the door.[122]

Ten years later the Richardsons were still living on West Street, although Thomas had completely changed career. He was now running the Prince of Wales, with children Thomas Jr and Minnie helping at the pub. Emma was also there, no doubt enjoying the

119 Death Register.
120 *Coventry Herald*, 31 May 1862.
121 Marriage Index, Q1 1863.
122 1881 Census.

sociable life of a landlord's wife.[123]

Thomas Richardson and daughter Minnie were still running the Prince of Wales in 1901, but Emma wasn't with them – she had died on 13 February 1900, coincidentally sixty-two years to the day since she had been baptised at Coventry's Holy Trinity.

123 1891 Census.

ANN LOLE

By necessity giving the most basic of information, a headstone never reveals the full story of a person's life. And, sometimes, that is a good thing – as in the following instance.

Born to ribbon weavers Daniel and Charlotte at Foleshill in 1831,[124] Ann Liggins had two marriages – one lasting less than a decade which very swiftly proved to be extremely unhappy, the other a loving coupling which lasted almost thirty years.

The fact that she would live to enjoy her second nuptials seemed extremely unlikely in April 1862, when she stood trial for murder.

Although she would not have entered into her marriage with William Lole had she known what the future would bring, nineteen year old Ann was no doubt beaming as she walked down the aisle at Foleshill Parish Church on 10 February 1850.[125] Both lived at Bell Green, and the twenty-two year old groom was a hand loom weaver.[126]

It didn't take long for things to go wrong. In August, just six months later, Ann resorted to calling her husband before the magistrates for failing to support her. After receiving a fine, William was compelled to make a payment to his already-estranged wife of 1s 3d each week.[127]

Matters took a turn for the worse months later when a son, Benjamin, was born. Still William Lole refused to support his family, a decision which early in the New Year saw him again appear before magistrates charged with neglect. Ann had been forced to apply to relieving officer Mr Bolton for support, at which point she

St Laurence, Foleshill
Courtesy Ian Rob/Creative Commons

and baby Benjamin were admitted to the workhouse.

William Lole was arrested and placed in the lock-up for a week to await an appearance in court. Magistrates heard that Ann had been given an amount of furniture by an uncle as a wedding gift, but Lole had sold it all to pay their rent.[128] With the money gone, he had abandoned his young family and moved back in with his parents and siblings at Bell Green.[129]

The weekly payments of 1s 3d stopped; Lole was once again brought before magistrates, on 15 May. Faced with a twenty-one day spell with hard labour at the County Gaol, the errant husband had a change of heart. He told the authorities that he was prepared to live with his wife again, and support his family. The case was adjourned for a fortnight to see whether he would adhere to the agreement.[130]

128 *Coventry Standard*, 10 January 1851.
129 1851 Census.

At just twenty, and having tasted life at the workhouse, Ann no doubt preferred this option, and the marriage seems to have blossomed once again. A son, William Jr, arrived in 1852, and another, Joseph, joined the family in 1857.[131]

In the midst of this domestic bliss, William Lole still occasionally graced the courts with his presence. In November 1855 he appeared on a charge of stealing a pocket handkerchief belonging to Frederick Barnet of Foleshill. Luckily for Lole, Mr Barnet declined to press the charge, and he was free to walk from the court.

But the scene of Lole's arrest by PC Willey revealed the new career he had begun, the Coventry officer apprehending the handkerchief thief at Victoria Colliery, Longford.[132]

The work at the colliery was fraught with danger. In May 1858 a youth named Swain suffered horrific injuries there when a quantity of coal fell through the roof and smashed his leg to just an extent that the shattered bones protruded through his trousers;[133] a similar fate befell a miner named Smith in September the same year, when falling coal fractured his thigh and caused other injuries.[134]

Two months later William Lole was the victim in another serious accident at the colliery, as reported in the *Coventry Times*:

> On Saturday last, a coroner's inquest was held at the Greyhound, Foleshill, before W.H. Seymour esq, coroner, on the body of William Lole. From the evidence it appears that deceased was engaged at work at the Victoria Colliery and, as he was not accustomed to work there, was cautioned as to the danger of riding up on the wagons. Unfortunately, however, his head came in contact with the roof of the pit, and his neck was dislocated, causing instantaneous death. After hearing the evidence, the Jury returned a verdict of Accidental Death. We are sorry to add the poor man has left a widow and family to deplore their loss.[135]

130 *Coventry Herald*, 16 May 1851.
131 Baptismal registers.
132 *Coventry Herald*, 16 November 1855.
133 *Coventry Times*, 12 May 1858.
134 *Coventry Herald*, 24 September 1858.

The press had evidently forgotten William Lole's earlier appearances before the authorities.

He was buried at St Laurence's, parish church of Foleshill, on 21 November 1858, aged thirty-one.[136]

Left behind were widow Ann, now twenty-seven, and sons Benjamin (seven), William Jr (five) and Joseph (one). The young family continued their lives as best they could, and by the time of the 1861 Census three years later they were still living at Bell Green, with head of the household Ann bringing in money as a ribbon weaver.

But that told just half the story – and the part which Ann presented in public.

MURDER OF A CHILD BY ITS MOTHER.

A shocking case of child murder, under circumstances of more than ordinary cruelty, has just occurred at the village of Foleshill, about a mile and a half from Coventry. The case has naturally created intense excitement in the neighbourhood, the alleged murderess being strongly suspected of having previously got rid of two other children to which she had given birth, by means of a similarly atrocious character.

The name of the accused is Ann Lole, widow of William Lole, a miner, of Foleshill, who died about three years ago. The woman had three children by her husband, who are still living, and since his death she has led a very immoral life. The result of her profligate habits has been the birth of no less than three illegitimate children. All of these have died within a brief period of their nativity. With regards to the death of the first two, all kinds of rumours are in circulation, and it is with the murder of the infant of which she was last delivered that the prisoner now stands charged.[137]

Baby Hannah Lole was born on Boxing Day, 1861. There is a

135 *Coventry Times*, 24 November 1858.

136 Burial register.

137 *Sheffield and Rotherham Independent*, 31 January 1862.

very good chance, therefore, that she had been conceived just weeks before the census of that year was taken. The identity of the father is unknown.

Mary Wagstaff, a neighbour at Bell Green, was called to the house the next day and saw the healthy newborn for the first time. But when she visited again four days later, on New Year's Eve, she noticed that the baby had a blister on the palm of her hand, and the skin was off on the back of the hand from her fingers to the wrist. There was a bit of coal in its left eye. The following morning Mrs Wagstaff called again, and discovered that a water-filled blister, the size of a shilling, had formed on the child's forehead, and the mark of a burst blister was on her left cheek. Two days later, to her horror, the neighbour saw that the skin was all off baby Hannah's face, and it was scabbed over.

Another neighbour, Matilda Atkins, saw the child two days before she died, and later gave horrific evidence at the trial of Ann Lole:

> Its brow was then scabbed and the face raw. The skin was off the left hand from the fingernails to the wrist. She saw the child on the next day, and when the prisoner undressed the child, by the advice of witness, to wash it, the skin came off with the clothes. Prisoner took up a pair of scissors and cut off a piece of skin that was loose. The back of the child was very sore. It appeared to witness that these appearances must be by scalding.

Dr Orton agreed, and told the court at Warwick Shire Hall that in his opinion the injuries had been caused by the "application of a hot liquid, and that there had been more than one application."

The inference was clear; Ann Lole had caused the death of her unexpected child by regular scalding. But defending counsel Mr Elers told the court that there had, in fact, been no murder – poor baby Hannah had died of natural causes. He suggested that, had there been any foul play, the last person a guilty person would go to was a medical man, and Ann Lole had indeed been to the doctor on a number of occasions.

The jury agreed. After deliberating for half an hour they returned a verdict of Not Guilty, and Ann Lole was allowed to leave.[138]

*

The truth of Hannah Lole's demise has never been established, nor has there been any corroborative evidence of the birth and untimely death of two other infants born to Ann Lole in the years since William's death in 1858; it just might have been unfounded malicious rumour after all.

The fact that Ann remained at Foleshill seems to indicate that she had nothing to hide, and she was certainly not going to run away.

On 24 August 1862 she married Thomas Cramp at St Laurence's, Foleshill. At twenty-four, Thomas was seven years her junior. Like her late first husband, he was also a miner.[139]

Almost a decade later, in the 1871 Census, the family are listed as living at Longford. Ann's three sons by William Lole were living at home, with Benjamin (now twenty-one) and William Jr (nineteen), like their stepfather finding work as miners, and fourteen year old Joseph working alongside his mother as a silk weaver. A new addition was three year old Francis, the son of Thomas and Ann.

In 1881 just Thomas, Ann and Francis remained at the family home, with the older boys now all married with families of their own.

Ann Cramp died in 1890, aged just fifty-eight, and was buried at St Laurence's on 19 February. It was where she had been married twice, and buried poor baby Hannah. Anyone browsing the headstones of the church's graveyard, and lighting upon those characters in this story, would remain blissfully unaware of the tragedy that lies behind the simple inscriptions.

138 *Coventry Weekly Times*, 2 April 1862.
139 Marriage certificate of Thomas Cramp and Ann Lole.

JOHN MARSTON

This is a tale of two marriages, one far happier than the other. The same bride walked down the aisle and, as we'll hear, her attitude to her second husband would have devastating consequences. But a parent would do anything to protect their child, wouldn't they?

Born at the end of 1816 to James and Martha Carpenter, little Frances was baptised at St Laurence's, Foleshill, on 9 February the following year.[140] She was recorded as 'Fanny', and despite appearing in some official documents as 'Frances', it seems probable that she went by the shortened version.

She was certainly listed as Frances when she married Thomas Payne on 28 December 1836, at the age of twenty.[141]

Although they were probably very much in love, a hint at the reason for their marriage is given in the baptismal record of their daughter Hannah, who was baptised on 21 May 1837 – five months after the nuptials.

Four years later, the census of 1841 records Hannah as being four years old, and a sister, Sophia, one. The family were living on Carpenter's Lane, Foleshill. Thomas, now thirty-two, was working as a ribbon weaver, as was his wife, now twenty-four.

Tragically, little Sophia died aged just three, and was buried at

---

140 Baptismal record of Fanny Carpenter.
141 Banns of Marriage between Thomas Payne and Frances Carpenter, dated 11, 18 and 25 December 1836.

St Laurence's on 28 January 1844. Worse was to come. Hannah followed months later, aged seven, and was buried with her sister on 17 March.[142]

Thomas and Fanny must have been devastated. But they began to rebuild their family, and in the spring of 1845 a son, William, was born. Another, Thomas Jr, arrived in the autumn of 1847. Young Thomas was baptised at St Paul's, Foleshill, on 31 March 1850.[143]

What should have been a very happy time for the Paynes soon turned to despair once again, when the boys' father Thomas died a year later, at the beginning of 1851. He was just forty-two years old.[144]

The immediate effect on Fanny and her sons was obvious. Just weeks later, on 30 March, the census for that year was taken, and the family are recorded as being at the home of Fanny's aunt Elizabeth Carpenter – her father's sister – although still on Carpenter's Lane.[145]

It had been a tumultuous fifteen years for Fanny. But worse – much worse – was to come.

*

John Marston was two years younger than Fanny Payne, but grew up in the same streets of Foleshill. He had been baptised at the same parish church on 10 May 1818, born to weavers Thomas and Mary Marston. He had an elder brother, William, born in 1817 – before the marriage of their parents – and two more soon followed: George, born in 1820, and James, in 1823.[146]

But once again, tragedy struck. Father Thomas died on 20 June 1824, wife Mary following on 10 November 1825.[147]

The boys were split up. By 1851 James was living as a lodger at the home of shoemaker John Smith, and working in the same trade;

---

142 Church of England Burials, 1813–1910.
143 Birth registers; Baptismal register of Thomas Payne.
144 Death register.
145 1851 Census.
146 Birth registers; Baptismal records.
147 Death registers.

George had relocated to Dudley, having married Elizabeth Pruston five years earlier.[148] Eldest brother William had married in 1845, to Mary Reeves.[149]

John Marston, now thirty-three, was living at the home of his aunt, Ann Marston, on Lockhurst Lane in Foleshill, further along the street from brother William and his young family. John was unmarried, and earning a living as a silk weaver.[150]

Magistrates would later hear that he had been attached to a young woman around this time, but when his advances were rejected he became morose. He had also been deeply affected by the sudden deaths of his parents – who, it was said, had themselves displayed symptoms on insanity from time to time. Since then John Marston had been in an almost permanent state of depression, and from time to time also acted strangely.[151]

Yet a chance for happiness would eventually come John's way. Living just half a mile from Carpenter's Lane,[152] and working in the same trade, at some point he met Fanny Payne.

They married at St Paul's, Foleshill, on Boxing Day 1859.[153] John was now forty-one years old and Fanny thirty-nine. Her sons Thomas and William were twelve and fourteen respectively.

John's happiness was complete when a daughter, Harriett, was born in December the following year. She was baptised at St Paul's on 31 March 1861.[154] That year's census, taken the following week, recorded the new family at Carpenter's Lane, with John, Fanny and William working as ribbon weavers, while Thomas was a shirt filler.

It should have been the happiest time of John Marston's life, and he was absolutely devoted to his little daughter. He later told police that he "loved her from the moment that she came into the world."

---

148 1851 Census; Wedding certificate of George Marston and Elizabeth Pruston.
149 Marriage record of William Marston and Mary Reeves.
150 1851 Census.
151 *Coventry Standard*, 15 August 1862.
152 Now Station Street East.
153 England Select Marriages, 1538–1973, FHL Film No. 991474.
154 Baptismal record of Harriett Marston.

But the nature of John and Fanny's marriage was not as it seemed from the outside. As the saying goes, no-one knows what goes on behind closed doors. Neighbours had heard arguments and crockery crashing inside the house, and John would later reveal to a police officer:

> My troubles have been very great. When anything is amiss at home my wife encourages her children to do as they like, and if I attempt to correct then, then she is angry with me. The child [Harriett] has been my sole care; she has occupied all my thoughts when I have been from home, and I thought if anything happened to me then they would throw their spite at her.[155]

This fear of harm coming to the light of his life drove his every waking moment, and would eventually lead to a horrifying conclusion.

*

Living next door to the Marstons on Carpenter's Lane was Charles Nichols and his wife.[156] They had sometimes heard disturbances through the wall, once a crash as though as table had fallen over.

On 8 May 1862, around ten o'clock in the morning, John Marston took little Harriett to visit Mr and Mrs Nichols. Charles asked the toddler, "Harriett, are you going 'a tat-ta'?," meaning for a walk, to which John replied "Yes." He said to his daughter, "Here, Harriett, kiss Mrs Nichols," and took the child over for the old lady to kiss.

Although it seemed to Mr Nichols that John was troubled, and appeared to have been crying, they went on their way happily enough.

Between ten and eleven o'clock a labourer named John Shaw was ploughing a field by the footpath leading from Carpenter's Lane to Whitmore Park. John Marston passed, little Harriett in his arms,

---

155 *Coventry Weekly Times*, 21 May 1862.
156 Almost certainly ribbon weavers Charles Nichols (b1780) and Susannah (b1796), who were living at Woodshire's Green, Foleshill at the time of the census the previous year.

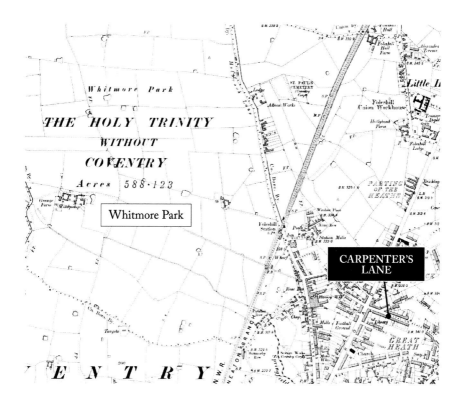

and the father drew his daughter's attention to the horses pulling the plough. It seemed to Shaw that the man was a devoted father, doing everything to please the child. They sat in the field for around twenty minutes, picking flowers.

Police Constable William Miller, on duty in Whitmore Park, also saw the happy father and daughter strolling in the sunshine. They were around three quarters of a mile from Carpenter's Lane, and the father seemed devoted to his daughter's happiness.

An hour or so later, Charles Nichols, the Marstons' next door neighbour, was in Cross Cheaping when he saw John Marston looking in to a shop window, but Harriett wasn't with him this time. He assumed the child had been taken home after their walk.[157]

When John didn't return home by the evening, wife Fanny went out looking for him and little Harriet. She found him in the

---

157 *Coventry Weekly Times*, 21 May 1862.

The Prince William Henry, Foleshill Road,
where John Marston was arrested
Courtesy www.HistoricCoventry.co.uk

Prince William Henry inn on the Foleshill Road, but the child was nowhere to be seen.[158]

The police were called, and Constable Joseph Knight arrived at the William Henry to find John and Fanny standing in the passage with the landlady, Mrs Ward. The group went into the parlour,

Fanny Marston asked her husband where Harriett was but received no reply; PC Knight asked the same question, and on seeing that the man was having difficulty answering asked the women to leave the room.

The moment they were gone, and the door closed, John Marston immediately confessed to the officer that he had fastened some yarn around Harriett's waist, tied a stone to it and then, putting some flowers in her hand, threw her into the pit.

Not unreasonably, Marston was arrested and taken to Longford

---

158 *Stroud Journal*, 24 May 1862.

Police Station, where he was taken into custody by Inspector Welch. The senior officer said he was being charged with the wilful murder of his daughter, and asked whether he had anything to say.

In response, John gave the following statement:

> I live in Carpenter's Lane, Foleshill. This morning, about eleven o'clock, I threw my little girl into a pit on Mr Berry's farm, in Whitmore Park. I tied a stone to it with some worsted. It is in a pit which has been fresh cleaned out. I will show the place if you will go with me. Her name is Harriett Marston. She is about eighteen months old. I did not do it on her account, but my wife's. I threw her into the pit near the footpath. I think it is in the second field, in the road going from Mr John Berry's house. I cannot write; I can read a little, but not write.

Inspector Welch read the statement back to him, and Marston confirmed it was accurate. The officer searched his prisoner, and found two pocket knives, a pair of scissors, a small cord and several pieces of string.

The Police then went out searching for little Harriett's body, going by John Marston's instructions. When they came back empty handed, the prisoner said he could show them the location to within a few feet.

Just after five o'clock the next morning Inspector Welch took Marston to Whitmore Park, on the way the prisoner telling the policeman how things were at home, and how he feared that something would happen to Harriett should he not be around to take care of her.

Welch later told the magistrates:

> We came to a place near a stile, where it appeared as though someone had been sitting on the grass, and some flowers lay about there. At this spot he became much affected, and rested himself on the stile, and remained there some four or five minutes. He seemed so much affected that I allowed him to indulge his feelings. He then pointed to some flowers that lay near, and made some remark, but what he said I am not clear about; they appeared to be fragments.
>
> It was a narrow path here, and he then walked on first, I following.

When he got to the next stile he appeared again much affected. When he got near the pit he turned from the footpath, and went up the hedge adjoining the pit.

He cried very much, and pointing over the hedge to the water said, "She lies just there."[159]

*

The inquest into Harriett's cause of death opened but was swiftly adjourned to allow the Police more time to continue their enquiries. The hearing resumed on 14 May at the Rose tavern on Lockhurst Lane, Foleshill, before Coroner A. Carter.

The first witness, Fanny Payne's son William. John Marston's stepson set the scene very well:

I left home on Thursday morning, at half-past eight, to go to my work; the accused was not there then. I returned at one o'clock; the deceased was not at home then, not my father-in-law [sic: stepfather]. On returning home at six o'clock I heard the news that my father had done away with the child, and went out to see if I could learn anything about it. At the request of my mother I went to Coventry to enquire if deceased had been left at the house of Mr Atkins, of Queen Street, Hillfields, a friend of my father[-in-law].

My father-in-law, and all of us, were very fond of the child; he was passionately fond of it. He showed his excessive love for the child by seeming always afraid of its being hurt.

Solicitor Mr Overall, watching proceedings on behalf of the prisoner, asked Coroner Carter whether it would be opportune to call some evidence showing the state of mind John Marston must have been in; Mr Carter replied that it was scarcely necessary, and that the magistrates' hearing would be the appropriate time.

The coroner then addressed the jury, reminding them that it was their sole duty to decide on the cause of death of Harriett Marston, not the mental condition of the her father at the time of her death; that was for another court to decide.

159 *Coventry Weekly Times*, 21 May 1862.

They returned a verdict of Wilful Murder against John Marston, who appeared to be not completely engaged with proceedings. He was removed to Coventry Gaol.

His demeanour was different when he was brought up before the magistrates, at Coventry's County Hall, with the reporter from the *Coventry Weekly Times* informing his readers:

> The prisoner, on entering the dock, seemed much reworn, serious, and thoughtful, and during the whole of the investigation appeared to listen attentively to the evidence. After he had been in the dock a few minutes he began crying, and was much distressed. The Bench considerately ordered a constable to place a chair in the dock, on which he sat during the examination.

Despite the deeply emotional nature of the case, the law had to run its course; and John Marston was committed to appear at the next Warwick Assizes.[160]

The trial opened on Saturday, 9 August, before Lord Chief Justice Baron Pollock. Further evidence was given as to the prisoner's melancholic demeanour, with his brother William testifying that John would often lie in bed all day without any apparent reason. Mary Brighton said she'd known John for twenty years, and he'd always exhibited a sad manner. He'd sometimes refuse food for a long period of time. "His mother was a person of strange character," she offered, in case it might help. As the prisoner heard about the discovery of his daughter's body he wept uncontrollably.

Justice Pollock's summing up reflected the underlying cause of Marston's actions, the judge telling the jury that the question that had to consider was whether the prisoner was sane or insane when he committed the fatal act. Justice Pollock revealed his own feelings on the matter, commenting that it seemed difficult to believe that the act had been committed otherwise than by a madman.

The jury agreed and returned a verdict of Not Guilty on the grounds of insanity.

John Marston was removed from the dock and taken to a secure

160 *Coventry Weekly Times*, 21 May 1862.

place, to be detained at Her Majesty's pleasure.[161]

*

Where John was taken is uncertain. The census of 1871 – nine years later – records him as an inmate at Broadmoor Lunatic Asylum for the Criminally Insane.

Broadmoor had been opened in 1863, with a secure wall enclosing its fifty-three acres. The first patient was a woman sent to the asylum on 27 May 1863 after she had killed her baby; the first male inmates arrived in February 1864, so it seems probable that John Marston was one of those first arrivals. In all likelihood he had spent eighteen months following the trial at Hatton Lunatic Asylum.

He was still there in 1881, and eventually died at the facility early in 1889. He was seventy-two years old;[162] his daughter should have been twenty-nine, with a family of her own.

Following the murder Fanny, the supposed root of all John's evils, continued living at Carpenter's Lane for another thirty-one years. Interestingly, in the census records of both 1871 and 1881 she gave her status as 'Married', and in 1891 she is listed as 'Widowed' – John having died two years earlier. At the time of the latter return she was living at the Carpenter's Lane home of son William Payne, his wife Maria and their eight children. Touchingly, one was named Harriet.[163]

---

161 *Warwickshire Standard*, 16 August 1862.
162 Death register: Q1, Berkshire, Vol 2c Page 272.
163 1871, 1881 and 1891 Census returns. Fanny Marston died in 1892 aged seventy–seven. She was buried at St Paul's, the scene of her two marriages, on 17 January 1893.

THOMAS CLARKE

The death of Thomas Payne at Victoria Colliery in 1851 – as we heard in the case of John Marston above – was tragic enough, but it would have paled compared to a catastrophic accident which almost happened there fifteen years later following the actions of a man who believed he had been wronged by a miner.

In 1866 John Turrall was forty-seven years old, and had already experienced both joy and tragedy in his life. Born in Foleshill in 1819, he was just twenty when he had married Eliza Ball at St Laurence's in December 1839. He was an engineer, and the twenty year old bride a weaver. Both lived at Longford, near the colliery[164] – in fact, just three doors along from the Cramp family,[165] whose son Thomas would marry Ann Lole following her acquittal of the murder of her daughter in 1862. Underlining the importance of the colliery to the area, John's father Charles Turrall was recorded on the marriage register as a coal dealer.

A daughter arrived in 1846, and was named Elizabeth after John's mother. The family probably looked ahead to a bright future.

But as ever in the Victorian era, dark clouds soon appeared. Eliza Turrall died late in 1848,[166] and with John working at the colliery, daughter Elizabeth was sent to live with her grandmother at Hurst

---

164 Wedding certificate of John Turrall and Eliza Ball.
165 1841 Census.
166 Death register.

Lane, Foleshill.[167]

John Turrall married for the second time on 31 May 1852. He was now thirty-three, and his new wife, Mary Parish, was just nineteen. Once again, the venue was St Laurence's, Foleshill.[168]

The newlyweds set about creating a home. John's daughter from his first marriage, Elizabeth, was baptised at St Laurence's on 28 November that year,[169] and over the years new additions joined the family; Ann was born in 1856, Charles in 1864, and Harriett on 20 September 1865.[170]

Life was good for the Turralls, and John was earning decent money at the Wyken Colliery.

But then, when little Harriett was just six months old, came an incident which threatened their happiness.

Unknown to John, on the 25th of March that year a man named Thomas Clarke – who had previously worked at the Wyken Colliery but some three years earlier had emigrated to America – had returned to Coventry to take care of some business.

A collier named John Swain had seen Clarke that evening, and he would later tell magistrates that he

> said he had a got a return ticket from America, but there was one b——d that he meant to shoot before he went back. I told him he must not talk in that way. He then said that Turrall was the cause of his being scalded some years ago, and he inquired at which pit Turrall worked. When I told him he said "I shall go and see." He showed me a revolver.

Two days later, on Tuesday 27 March 1866, John Turrall was working in the engine house at Wyken Colliery.

Thomas Clarke arrived at the works just after 1.00pm and approached the banksman, William Hewitt, pointing a gun at his chest. The colliery worker told him to step back from the mouth of

---

167 1851 and 1861 Census returns.
168 Marriage register, 1852. Mary Parish's age from census returns.
169 Baptismal record.
170 1939 Register of England and Wales.

the pit, as there was a cage coming up containing a number of men.

Hewitt shouted "Hold!" in the direction of the engine room, and watched as Clarke turned and walked towards the building.

John Turrall, working inside, would later testify:

> I saw the prisoner come up the engine house steps with a gun upon his shoulder. He was holding it by the stock. He walked towards me. I was there stranding upon a raised block, about six inches high.
>
> The prisoner half-cocked the gun, then full-cocked it, and fired it at me. The shots struck me on the left side of the neck. There have been five shots taken out of my neck this week, and more remain there.
>
> After the shot was fired I went to the corner of the engine house for half a minute, and then returned and drew the men up the pit. I had previously received a signal to stop, and it was just as I had stopped the engine that the shot was fired.
>
> I produce the smock which I was wearing at the time, in which there is a hole made by the shots. I bled a little from the wound.
>
> I know the prisoner. He was working with me five or six years ago. He was a stoker. He did not say anything to me before he fired the gun. We were friends when he left this country. I don't know of any motive the prisoner could have in shooting at me.[171]

Turrall's almost nonchalant testimony belies the fact that, had it not been for his prompt response to William Hewitt's shouted warning, his being shot by Clarke would have resulted in the cage containing six men slowly making its way to the surface hurtling back down the shaft to their certain doom.

Hewitt heard the shot fired, and a youth named Charles Watts ran out of the engine room, shouting "He has shot old Jack!" Another man, engine cleaner Benjamin Hewitt, had been in the engine room when the trigger had been pulled and later told magistrates that Clarke had been just a yard and a half from Turrell at the time. Despite this, one shot put out the glass of a window.

PC Phipps soon arrived, and apprehended Thomas Clarke in the

171 *Coventry Standard*, 7 April 1866.

engine room. He told the officer,

> I don't care a damn for you or the charge either. I am an American soldier, and mean to give it all the English b——ds before I go back again. Nor do I care about being hung.[172]

Unsurprisingly, Clarke was committed to trial at the next Warwick Assizes, three months later, at the Shire Hall. The hearing was before Mr Justice Mellor,[173] with Mr Leigh appearing for the prosecution and Mr Elers for the defence.[174]

Commenting that Clarke was a 'rough-looking fellow', a reporter from the *Birmingham Daily Post* remarked that, as the judge sentenced him to six years for unlawfully wounding, his Honour added that "altogether he [Clarke] appeared to be a man utterly regardless of the value of human life."[175]

*

As the angry Clarke served his time, John Turrall recovered and – despite being fifty years old – set about adding to his family. Daughter Hannah was born in 1869, and another son, John Jr, joined the family the following year.

The census of 1871 records them as living at Hurst Lane, Foleshill, next door to John's mother Elizabeth. He is listed as an engine driver, with Mary proudly telling the enumerator that she was an 'engine driver's wife'. Of their children, fifteen year old Ann was working as a weaver, while Charles (seven) and Harriett (five) were at school. Hannah and John, just two and one years old, no doubt kept their mother busy at home.

John Turrall died in 1874; he was fifty-five years old.[176] The family continued to live at the same house on Hurst Lane, and son

172 *Coventry Standard*, 7 April 1866.
173 *Coventry Herald*, 13 July 1866.
174 *Coventry Standard*, 13 July 1866.
175 *Birmingham Daily Post*, 12 July 1866.
176 Death register.

Charles followed him into the mining industry.[177] He would marry and raise a family of his own, and by the time of the 1911 Census was operating as a coal dealer.

Harriett Turrall, just six months old when her father was almost killed, went on to live a long and happy life. In March 1889, at the age of twenty-three, she married William Grimley at St Laurence's, where her father had himself married twice. Perhaps unsurprisingly, William was a miner.[178]

A snapshot of their life together was provided in 1911, when the census of that year showed they had been married for twenty-two years and had welcomed five children, four of whom had survived into adulthood. William was still working as a miner.

In 1939, when the Register of England and Wales was taken, Harriett and William were still together. They were residing at 17 Lady Lane, Longford, close by where they had both lived all their lives.

Harriett died the following spring, aged seventy-four, and William in 1945, aged seventy-nine.[179]

Nothing is known of the murderous Thomas Clarke following his discharge from prison; it is probable that he returned to America to resume his Fenian sympathies.

177 1881 Census.
178 Marriage certificate of William Henry Grimly and Harriett Turrall.
179 Death registers.

THOMAS BAKER

There are many people over the centuries who have felt themselves trapped into wedlock, but few have resorted to attempted murder to avoid a walk down the aisle, as was the case in our next story.

Henrietta Westley was twenty-one years old when she gave birth to an illegitimate daughter, Ellen, at the end of 1865 at Coventry Union Workhouse. The father, Thomas Baker, was the same age. Both worked in the textile industry, and came from respectable families.

While other fathers may have kicked their daughter out of their home for bringing shame on the family, William Westley was protective and provided shelter for Henrietta and his young granddaughter.[180] Perhaps it was the forthcoming nuptials which swayed his mind.

But when the young couple were still unmarried by the Easter of 1867, even the patient Mr Westley must have wondered what Thomas Baker's intentions were, despite his frequent promises to make Henrietta an honest woman.

On the morning of Monday, 8 April 1867 Baker called at the Westley house on Bayley Lane and repeated his promise. Henrietta no doubt took this with a pinch of salt, for he had never even visited

---

180 Birth and baptismal records of Ellen Westley; Baptismal records of Thomas Baker and Henrietta Westley; Census returns. The 1861 Census records Thomas Baker as a silk dyer, and Henrietta Westley as a silk winder.

Bayley Lane, with County Hall far right

Mr Green's beerhouse, officially 'the Nugget'
Courtesy www.HistoricCoventry.co.uk

the church and put up the Banns. Nevertheless, the couple were still romantically involved and she agreed to join him for a walk.

They went first to Mr Pickering's on the High Street, where she had a glass of gin while Baker enjoyed a whiskey, and then strolled along Hill Street, past St Osburg's Catholic Church, and then along Coundon Road and Barker's Butts Lane to Coundon. It started to rain so they went into a hovel, emerging shortly after to continue their walk together. Suddenly Baker produced a pistol from the pocket inside his coat, and showed it to Henrietta without saying a word. He made no answer when she asked what he planned to do with it, instead silently putting it away.

They continued to the beer house run by Thomas Green on Coundon Green, where they had more drinks.[181] Mrs Green later told magistrates that she remembered the couple; she had overhead Baker suggesting that should the rain continue they would only

---

181 *Coventry Standard*, 3 May 1867. Green's beer house was named the Nugget, and replaced by a larger premises of the same name in 1966. Thomas Green had apparently been to the Australian goldmines, perhaps returning with the funds to purchase the house.

walk as far as Allesley, but if it stayed dry they could take a train to Birmingham. Henrietta indignantly refused, saying he'd never catch her going there.[182]

Henrietta would later tell the court what happened when they left Mr Green's:

> On coming out I felt unwell. We went down to the lane, and I laid my head upon his shoulder, and told him I felt bad. I then felt something like a blow on the face, and until I saw blood I did not know I had been shot. I fell down and became insensible.[183]

Miraculously, Henrietta's life was spared because the ball had dropped out of the barrel of the pistol. Instead, her severe injuries were caused by the powder and wadding, the weapon being so close to her face.[184]

The right jawbone was broken, close to its angle, and all the back teeth on the left side had been knocked out.[185]

Labourer George Yateman was working in a field near the lane, and heard the report of a pistol. He then saw a man running away from the sound.

Henrietta was unconscious for just a few seconds; as she came to she saw Baker running up the lane, and called out "Tom", at which he turned and came back, and the couple kissed and embraced. Baker helped Henrietta to her feet, and the couple walked slowly towards Allesley, where they stopped at a nearby house to seek help.[186]

Eighteen year old Elizabeth Grimes opened the door, and was shocked by the appearance of the blood-soaked woman. Both of the visitors appeared to have been drinking. She called her father, Daniel Grimes, who declined Baker's request to call a doctor and told them to go.

At a neighbouring house they saw a man named Henry Cross

182 *Coventry Herald and Free Press*, 3 May 1867.
183 *Coventry Standard*, 3 May 1867.
184 *Cork Constitution*, 3 May 1867.
185 *Illustrated Weekly News*, 4 May 1867.
186 *Coventry Standard*, 3 May 1867.

working in the garden; he called to his employer inside, who came out and told Cross to take them to the nearby home of PC Tomkins,[187] who immediately noticed a hole in Henrietta's cheek. There were no flies on this constable. She was covered with blood, and Tomkins asked Thomas Baker who had shot her. His reply was to tell the constable that was nothing to do with him, and instead asked him to put her to bed and call a doctor. Not surprisingly, PC Tomkins charged Baker with the shooting, and on searching him found a pistol, a bullet, some caps and some gunpowder. He took his prisoner and poor Henrietta by cab to Coventry Police Station, paid for with money found in Baker's pocket.[188]

On arrival at Coventry Thomas Baker was locked up. He was extremely excitable, and his hand was swollen and burnt, apparently by gunpowder. He was taken to the cells, and watched overnight by an officer. Henrietta told the Coventry officers that she believed she had been struck and then shot, and as if to illustrate the point spat some blood out of her mouth onto the floor. A tooth followed. She was sent to the Coventry and Warwickshire Hospital.

The following morning Baker asked how Henrietta was – would she get over it? On being told that the officer on duty was unable to say, he replied "She's shot in the head with a bullet."[189]

*

Thomas Baker's appearance before the magistrates at Coventry's County Hall was delayed several times as Henrietta's poor health prevented her from attending to give evidence. When she finally appeared, on Friday, 26 April, the exit wound on her left cheek was plastered up, and she appeared very ill.[190]

Having heard her evidence, and that of others corroborating her story, the magistrates had no hesitation in sending Thomas Baker to trial at the next Warwick Assizes, on the charge of attempted

187 *Coventry Herald*, 3 May 1867.
188 *Coventry Herald*, 19 April 1867.
189 *Coventry Herald*, 3 May 1867.
190 *Leeds Mercury*, 29 April 1867.

murder. The prisoner said he hadn't intended to shoot her.

At the Shire Hall, on 19 July 1867, Henrietta testified that Baker had been kind to her before and after the incident, and was genuinely concerned for her welfare. The judge concurred, and interrupted the trial to tell the jury that the prisoner's actions after the shooting were not those of a man who intended murder. The jury agreed, and without hearing any further evidence returned a verdict of Not Guilty.[191]

The fact that Thomas Baker was drunk at the time of the shooting had weighed heavy on the minds of both judge and jury, who apparently believed that the pistol had gone off accidentally while in his coat pocket.

But if that was the case, why were there burn marks on Baker's hand? He must have had his hand on the weapon at the time of the shooting – for what purpose?

*

Despite the shooting incident, Henrietta Westley and Thomas Baker appear to have remained together. Although his name disappears into the mists of time, his presence hangs heavy in Henrietta's life over the next couple of years; a son, Thomas – perhaps named after his father – was born at the workhouse on 22 May 1868, ten months after the trial, but sadly didn't live long. He was baptised at St Michael's on 21 August – recorded as being illegitimate, with no father named – and died days later, being buried at Coventry's London Road Cemetery on 27 August.[192]

Perhaps the short, tragic life of her son weighed on Henrietta's mind, for the following month – on 7 September 1868 – Ellen, her daughter with Thomas Baker, was baptised at St Michael's. She was now nearly three years old, and was also recorded as being illegitimate.[193]

In April 1871 Henrietta once again stood at St Michael's for

191 *Leamington Spa Courier*, 20 July 1867.
192 Baptismal record and Death register of Thomas Westley.
193 Baptismal record of Ellen Westley.

the baptism of a child, this time son William, who had been born on 4 November 1870 at St John Street. Once again no father was named,[194] but if this was Thomas Baker he was not to enjoy Henrietta's company for much longer.

When the census was taken two weeks before William's baptism, the enumerator recorded the Westley family at 34 St John Street. Henrietta, now twenty-seven but for some reason listed as being twenty-five, was employed as a silk winder, as was her sister Emma. Brother Thomas was working as a porter, and youngest sister Sarah Ann, just twelve, was at school. They lived under the roof of their parents, William and Sarah, and also with the family were Henrietta's surviving children, five year old Ellen and William, four months. They were euphemistically recorded as the niece and nephew, rather than the grandchildren, of head of the household William.

But Henrietta was soon to meet a much more reliable partner than the trigger-happy Thomas Baker.

Another son, Thomas Taylor Westley, was born in 1873. His year of birth is taken from census returns, for there is no apparent baptism record; but in 1881 he is listed as living at Well Street with his father Thomas Taylor, a thirty-three year old whitesmith, mother Henrietta and half-brother William. Half-sister Ellen was living at the home of Sarah Bell, two doors down, working as a silk winder.[195]

Another daughter, named Henrietta after her mother, was born on 23 July 1882 and baptised at St Michael's that October. Although no father is listed on the register, the father was almost certainly Thomas Taylor.[196] Sadly, he died the following year.

Henrietta passed away in the spring of 1888, aged just forty-four. She was buried at the London Road Cemetery on 23 April.[197]

I wonder whether her children grew up asking their mother what

---

194 Baptismal record of William Garland Westley.
195 1881 Census.
196 Baptismal register of Henrietta Westley.
197 Death registers; Burial records.

had happened to her face. Did she invent some accident, or tell the truth and warn them of getting involved with the wrong sort of person?

APRIL 1872

DAVID OLDHAMS

St Laurence, the parish church of Foleshill, features in many of the stories in this volume. And it was the venue for the marriage, in August 1825, of the victim in this case, and the union which would in time produce the murderer.

John Oldhams and Sarah Copson were both in their early twenties and employed as ribbon weavers when they exchanged vows at St Laurence's.[198]

Four children were born to the couple; Elizabeth in 1826, David in 1829, John Jr in 1832 and Sarah Jr in 1834.[199]

Frustratingly, there is very little in the way of official records for the family. David Oldhams was baptised at St Laurence's on 27 June 1838, when he was approaching his eighth birthday, and his siblings appear in the census three years later.

At that time, they were living on Paradise Row,[200] next door to Sarah Oldhams' widowed father Samuel Copson. There was very little of a paradise about their lives. John Oldhams is missing from the census; he had died at some point between the birth of his youngest daughter in 1834 and the census taking in 1841, when Sarah is recorded as a widow, but no record can be found.

And while his children Elizabeth (fifteen), David (eleven), John

198 Marriage record of John Oldhams and Sarah Copson, 30 August 1825.
199 Dates taken from ages recorded in the 1841 Census.
200 Paradise Row was later renamed Eden Street.

(eight) and Sarah (six) are recorded in 1841 alongside their mother, apart from the eldest son there are no confirmed records of any of them afterwards – no marriage or death record. There is a John Oldhams who was convicted at Warwick Assizes of larceny, being sentenced to four years' imprisonment, there is no guarantee that this was the son of John Sr and Sarah.[201]

Things seemed to have settled by the dawn of the 1860s, for Sarah Oldhams and her son David are recorded as living at Cromwell Street. She was by now fifty-eight, a widow working as a silk winder. David was thirty, an unmarried silk weaver.[202]

Ten years later they had moved to Brick Kiln Lane,[203] both undertaking the same work. David was still unmarried, aged forty-two, and Sarah about to turn seventy.

In a row of houses full of people engaged in the textile industry, their neighbours included Ann and David Phillips, twenty-eight and twenty-seven, and their three young daughters who lived next door; Caroline and William Warren, both in their sixties and their three grown up children; and Alfred and Sarah Birch, both thirty-eight, who lived nearby with their six children ranging from thirteen years to three months.[204]

All of these people were going about their business as usual, when around half-past eight on the evening of 2 March 1872 Ann Phillips heard screaming and groaning coming from the house next door, at which the Oldhams lived. She went outside and stood by the front door, listening to the noises coming from within, and amid the screams thought she heard someone struggling on the floor. Rightly concerned, Mrs Phillips went through the passageway and into the rear yard to seek help; there she saw Caroline Warren, who had been sitting by her fireplace when she too heard the screams.

The two women knocked on the door of nearby Alfred Birch, who

---

201 England & Wales Criminal Registers, Warwickshire, 1854.
202 1861 Census.
203 Brick Kiln Lane was renamed Gulson Road in 1905. See the *Coventry Evening Telegraph* of 8 April 1905.
204 1871 Census.

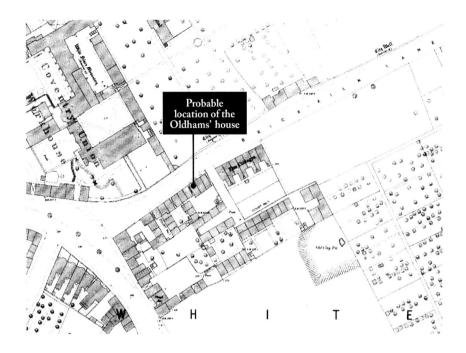

Probable location of the Oldhams' house

went with them to investigate.

The front door was closed, but only on the latch; Mr Birch flicked it open and entered the room, which was in darkness, and now silent.

Adjusting to the gloom, Birch heard a noise and thought he recognised the voice as that of David Oldhams. He walked towards the sound, and took the man by the wrists. Mrs Warren and Mrs Phillips came into the room, the latter holding a candle, and Birch was now able to see that David Oldhams' hands and forearms – which he still had hold of – were covered in blood, as were his clothes. He seemed rational but excited, and said to Alfred, "Oh dear, dear, Mr Birch, I have killed my mother."

The women turned their attention to Sarah Oldhams, who was sitting in a chair with her back to a table which was against one blood-spattered wall. She was unconscious, her face covered with blood which was running freely from a large wound above her left eye. Their first thought was that she was dead.

With Alfred Birch continuing to maintain a firm grip on David Oldhams, the women sent for the police, with Constable Knight arriving at the scene just before nine o'clock. By this time there was a house full of people, and Mrs Oldhams had been placed on a bed in the front part of the house.

The officer asked, to nobody in particular, "Who has done this?" David piped up "I have murdered my mother." When he further said that he'd done it with his fists, PC Knight took one look at the cuts on Sarah's face and remarked, "Fists could not do that."

He took David into custody, and set off for Longford Police Station. On the way they stopped at the house of Dr John Orton, who examined the prisoner and confirmed that, although his hands were smeared with blood, they were not swollen as they would have been had he beaten his mother with them, and there was no abrasion of the skin.

Constable Knight then took his prisoner to the station where he was questioned by Inspector Olliver, following which the more experienced officer went to the Brick Kiln Lane and examined the scene of the crime.

The room had a pool of blood on the floor, and a piece of candle which had been trampled underfoot was found lying at the end of the fireplace fender. Having searched the entire house, Olliver came to the conclusion that the only object that might have caused the cuts to Sarah Oldham's face was an iron candlestick which, although not bloody, had a sharp enough base to have inflicted the wounds. Dr Orton later agreed that it was a possible weapon.

When David Oldhams was asked why he had carried out such a brutal assault upon his mother, he said he did not know. He hadn't been drinking, and admitted he "must have been possessed".[205] Inspector Olliver would later tell the coroner's inquest that during Oldham's time in custody he had displayed signs of insanity.

On Friday, 8 March the prisoner was brought up before magistrates Morris and Gulson at Coventry's County Hall. The hearing wasn't a long one; prosecutor Mr Neale told the bench that Mrs Oldhams was too ill to attend, so a remand of one week was granted.[206]

As it transpired, Sarah would never recover, and she died on

205 *Coventry Standard*, 22 March 1872.
206 *Coventry Standard*, 15 March 1872.

The Royal Oak,
scene of the inquest into Sarah Oldhams' death

the morning of 16 March. An inquest was hastily convened for that afternoon before coroner Mr Dewes at the Royal Oak on Gosford Street, where the inquiry into Elizabeth Kington's death at the hands of her husband had been carried out thirteen years earlier. Dr Orton, who had examined Sarah following the attack and then attended to her at the hospital every day since, would tell the coroner that apart from a few moments where she appeared semi-conscious, the poor old lady had never regained her senses.[207] Sarah Oldhams was buried at St Laurence's two days later.[208]

Dr Orton's description of the wounds at the inquest was harrowing:

> There was a punctured wound over the deceased's left eye, extending about 2½ inches backwards. There were two incised clean wounds under the left eye, a jagged wound on the lip, and two loose teeth. There was a considerable amount of swelling all round the neck, which in my opinion was caused by severe pressure. There was a large bruise on the chest, and many bruises on other parts of the body, particularly on her hands and arms, as if she had held them out to defend herself.
>
> There was much haemorrhage from one of the arteries of the left eye, which bled for several days. The blood which was seen about must have come from the wounds on the forehead and near the

207 *Coventry Standard*, 22 March 1872.
208 Church of England Burials, 1813–1910: Foleshill, St Laurence.

left eye.[209]

The motive was uncertain; Ann Phillips, who had entered the blood-spattered house with Alfred Birch and Caroline Warren, said she had lived near the Oldhams for three years, and did not think there was any ill-feeling between mother and son. "I have heard David abuse her when drunk, but he was kind and affectionate when sober," she told the coroner. Mrs Warren agreed, saying she had never heard David threaten his mother; Mr Birch had never even heard them have a quarrel.[210]

Despite this, given the fact that only mother and son had been in the house, and he had confessed to the attack, the inquest jury wasted no time in returning a verdict of Wilful Murder against David Oldhams.

Perhaps his claim to have been 'possessed' when he carried out the brutal attack on his mother had been accurate; he failed to appear at the inquest to hear the charge against him due to his weakened mental state and, despite the inquest jury's verdict that he be tried for murder, it was clear he would never be fit to take his place in the dock before either magistrates or trial judge.

On 8 April David Oldhams was admitted to Broadmoor Criminal Lunatic Asylum on the orders of the Secretary of State,[211] recorded as inmate 64155. He never saw the outside of its walls again, and died there on 5 February 1879.[212]

209 *Coventry Standard*, 22 March 1872.
210 *Coventry Herald*, 22 March 1872.
211 UK Calendar of Prisoners, 1868–1929.
212 UK Lunacy Patients Admissions Registers, 1846–1921.

EDWARD EAST

When I lead my 'Coventry's Victorian Murder Mile' walking tour around the city centre and relate various tales of gruesome goings-on from the past – some from this volume – I often remark that the tour should be subtitled "It wasn't a happy marriage…", because more often than not that is the root of many evils, as you will surely realise having got this far, dear Reader.

While most marry for love, others, sadly, can thank unexpected pregnancies or a greedy eye on an inheritance as the reason for walking down the aisle.

The following case belongs to the latter category.

Sarah Hales was married to George, who had for many years worked as a ribbon weaver,[213] and lived on Hood Street. At the time of the 1861 census both husband and wife were twenty-seven years old, and living with them was Sarah's sister Eliza Butlin, two years younger.

Through thriftiness and perseverance George managed to save enough from his meagre earnings to open a haberdashery shop, and the young couple no doubt looked forward to the future with great excitement.

But then, not long after opening the new venture George died, on 21 September 1863. He was just twenty-eight.[214]

---

213 1851 and 1861 census returns.
214 Date of death from headstone.

At least widow Sarah was provided for, with the shop and business being transferred into her name. Her future looked rosy when she met Edward East, nine years her junior, who was the son of William East who ran the Craven Arms Inn on Coventry's High Street. It was a respectable match. The couple became engaged.

But the reality of life in the Victorian era once again claimed a victim. Before they could be married, Sarah became afflicted with a terminal illness, and although her sister Eliza and fiancé Edward nursed her as best they could,[215] Sarah died on 31 December 1869. She was thirty-six, and was buried with her husband at Coventry's London Road Cemetery on 5 January 1870.[216]

Sarah and Eliza's widowed mother, seventy year old Sarah Butlin, moved into the Hood Street premises, with Eliza running the shop, which she had inherited from her sister.[217]

The regular visits to the house by Edward East during his time with Sarah Hales had resulted in an attachment between he and Eliza. Or was it that he was attached to the property?

After a year of courtship they were married at All Saints, Birmingham on 31 August 1871,[218] and East moved into the Hood Street premises, no doubt thinking he now had a business under his control as well as a wife.

But the new Eliza East was made of sterner stuff; on the day of their wedding a quarrel had taken place when Edward discovered he would not have any say on the running of the business, and an unhappy life followed. Assaults and threats became commonplace, and after just a few months the couple were separated.

He spent some time living at the home of a Mr Butler on Earl Street, and it was because of this arrangement that things came to a head between husband and wife.

On 28 July 1874 Eliza sued Mr Butler for non-payment of an invoice for drapery supplied to him for the amount of £1 18s 10d.

215 *Warwick, Warwickshire and Leamington Gazette*, 1 August 1874.
216 Date of death from headstone; Burial record.
217 1871 Census.
218 Marriage certificate of Edward East and Eliza Butlin.

To her surprise, Mr Butler produced a receipt for the amount claimed, having paid the money to her husband, Edward East. She had not authorised him to collect her debts, but the matter was dropped despite Eliza telling the court that "her husband was a drunken bad man, that she had separated from him, and under a deed of separation the debts and business were to be hers."[219]

Edward East left the court humiliated, and determined to have some measure of revenge. The following day, he intended to do exactly that.

*

On the afternoon of Wednesday, 29 July 1874 Edward East walked into the shop of John Salmons, a general dealer, at 9 New Buildings.[220] Mr Salmons' wife Maria was at the counter, and he asked to see a pistol. As he viewed a selection he commented that a friend who was going out to New Zealand wanted a total of six weapons.

Mrs Salmons sold East one pistol for 3s, but as she didn't sell bullets he was obliged to go elsewhere.

The customer then went to the shop of gunsmith John Newark, of 27 Bailey Lane,[221] where Mrs Harriett Newark sold him half a pound of large shot.

Trouble was brewing.

At around half-past eight that evening ribbon weaver George Yardley – who knew Edward East by sight – saw him walking along Raglan Street, seemingly in the direction of his estranged wife's home on Hood Street.

Mr Yardley entered the street first, and ahead saw Eliza East and her mother standing outside their house in conversation with Richard Allen and his wife, acquaintances who lived on East Street. Mr Yardley stopped and joined the friendly chat.

219 *Warwick, Warwickshire and Leamington Gazette*, 1 August 1874.
220 Address from 1861, 1871 and 1881 census returns.
221 Address from 1871 and 1881 census returns.

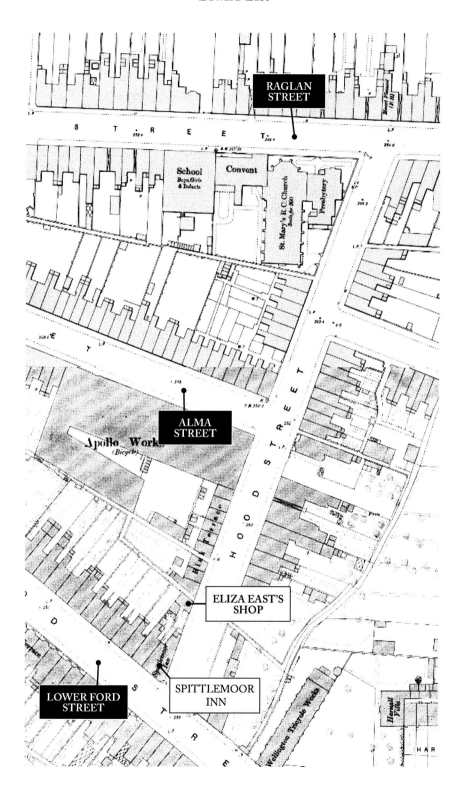

RAGLAN STREET

School Boys Girls & Infants

Convent

St. Mary's R.C. Church *Seats for 360*

Presbytery

ALMA STREET

Apollo Works *(Bicycle)*

ELIZA EAST'S SHOP

SPITTLEMOOR INN

LOWER FORD STREET

Richard Allen looked up and saw Edward East tentatively walking along Hood Street. He came halfway down the street and made as though about to turn right into Alma Street, but stopped and waited for a minute, apparently undecided what to do.

Mr Yardley also noticed East, and watched as he approached the group with his hands in his jacket pockets. Rather than joining in the conversation – he would most certainly have been an unwelcome guest – East stopped and stood behind Allen and Yardley, staring into the window of his estranged wife's shop.

Just then the front door slammed shut in the breeze, and presented a natural ending to the conversation. Mr Yardley began to walk off, as did Mr Allen. Eliza, behind them, walked for a few yards with Mrs Allen, intending to go to the back door.

Suddenly the men heard the report of a gun, and turned to see that Eliza East had been shot in the face. Richard Allen immediately struck Edward East, who staggered against the wall and fell to the pavement. George Yardley shouted "Dick, look out, there's a pistol in his hand!"

A quantity of wadding, on fire, fell from the pistol and Yardley was able to wrest the weapon from East's grasp.

Police Sergeant Gregory, on duty nearby, heard the gunshot and looked down Hood Street to see a man on the floor. The officer approached, arriving on the scene in time to see Eliza going to the doorway of her house with her hands to her face, blood streaming through her fingers onto her chest.

He was told that the man on the floor – Edward East – had just shot his wife.

Sergeant Gregory was handed the pistol by Mr Yardley, and took East into custody. As the two of them started walking towards the Police station, not a word was spoken until, a hundred yards along, East volunteered "She forced me to do it." Three hundred yards further still he suddenly exclaimed, "I'm going to have a fit!" then fell to the floor as a violent seizure took hold of him.

On arrival at the station Sergeant Gregory first sent for a doctor to visit Eliza at Hood Street, then searched his prisoner. He found a quantity of shot – the officer believed they were No. 1 shots – some caps, powder, and a bit of wool evidently used as wadding.

East was not in a fit state to be questioned or formally charged that night, so was placed in a cell overnight to recover.

Doctors William Dresser and John Brown arrived at Hood Street around nine o'clock and examined Eliza. Dr Brown would later tell magistrates:

> I found her suffering from gunshot wounds in the face. I found on the left cheek six shot holes, which were then bleeding. Dr Dresser had joined me. We also found one shot hole on the left ear and three on the nose; the one on the left penetrating the cartilage and septum of the nose, and grazing the upper lip; two on the forehead, and one near the temporal artery; another other the left eyebrow, and one on the right cheek.
>
> Dr Dresser joined me and this is our joint report. We found the two shots produced, one on the inside of the left cheek, the other on the right cheek. The one on the left cheek had penetrated through and was found inside the mouth against the gums. The other shot produced has been extracted since. We also found a shot mark on the point of the left shoulder. There are five more shots to be extracted.
>
> The shot in the ear ran along the mastoid portion of the temporal bone. Had it gone direct instead of meeting with that bone, it must have killed her. The shots not extracted were too deep for us to get at them. They are coming now to the surface. Altogether I should think there were twelve or thirteen shot penetrations. Mrs East was in danger for some time after she had been shot, in consequence of the wounds I have described.

Eliza's precarious health caused several delays to the magistrates' hearing, during which time the case against her husband was made clear. He was in time committed to trial at Warwick.[222]

The Assizes, which opened before Mr Justice Denham on Monday, 19 December, had a busy calendar. Cases included the murder in Birmingham of Samuel Earp by fifteen year olds John Kelly and Patrick Sullivan; George Osborne for the murder of

222 *Coventry Standard*, 14 August 1874.

his wife Suzannah at Stretton-on-Dunsmore; and James Hayes, charged with the murder of John Rowley on Coventry's Spon Street – the case we'll read about next.

On the same list was Edward East. The prisoner was in a poor condition, spending much of the hearing sobbing into a handkerchief which he had placed over his face, and the court heard that he had undergone several surgical operations for a fistula.[223]

Sentenced to twenty years for attempted murder, the admission record of Edward East upon his entry to Parkhurst Prison gives a full physical description of the wastrel. He was 5ft 3in tall, of slender build, with grey hair and hazel eyes. The 'distinguishing marks' column added further information on his delicate injury; "Scar nose and right wrist, testicles wasted, right thumb-nail split."[224]

*

Edward East served sixteen of his twenty years, all at Parkhurst, and was recorded in the 1881 Census as a convict, formerly a commercial traveller in the ribbon trade. On 13 January 1891 he was discharged, heading to Birmingham and a prison system-assisted rehabilitation.[225]

Frustratingly, there appears to be no record of him in either the 1891 or 1901 census records, so we are unable to say anything about his life following his release. All we know for certain is that he died at Warwick at the end of 1908;[226] had he attempted a reconciliation with Eliza?

Of the victim in this story, no more can be found. Perhaps not surprisingly Eliza East disappeared from the newspapers, but no further record – a census entry or death – can be found for either Eliza East or Eliza Butlin.

223 *Coventry Herald*, 18 December 1874.
224 Criminal Registers, MEPO 6/003/00061.
225 Criminal Registers, MEPO 6/003/00061.
226 Death Register.

114

JAMES HAYES

Our final story in this collection is a familiar tale; a group of people out drinking at their local. The alcohol kicks in, tempers flare and arguments ensue. A scene most reading this will have witnessed for themselves. But I'd wager that very few, if any, concluded as did this case from 1874.

Charles Jones, thirty-two, had been landlord of the Black Swan on the corner of Spon Street and Barras Lane for just six months, and he and wife Sarah no doubt getting used to the locals when, on 22 September, a group of drinkers from along the street at Court No. 30 had spent the evening in the front room of his inn.[227]

But this wasn't a friendly group enjoying a night out.

Hannah Miller, a fifty-four year old widow[228] who had been the common-law wife of fifty-five year old John Rowley for over twenty years, and who lived at 2 House in the court,[229] was sitting with John and their friends Mr and Mrs Frederick Cotton when Mrs Elizabeth Hayes from 4 House[230] came into the room, and her husband James popped his head around the door to see who was

---

227 The licence for the Black Swan was transferred to Charles Jones from William Mason. [*Coventry Standard*, 27 March 1874.]. Age and name of Mrs Jones taken from 1881 Census, which reveals Charles Jones had taken over the licence of the Plough on Spon Street.

228 1871 Census.

229 The couple had lived at House 2 Court 30 at least since the 1861 Census, thirteen years earlier, and probably more.

230 First name and address from 1871 Census.

The Black Swan, on the corner of Spon Street and Barras Lane
Courtesy www.HistoricCoventry.co.uk

there before heading into the kitchen.

There was bad blood between Mrs Hayes and Hannah Miller; for over a year, some misunderstanding had caused tension between the two. After Elizabeth Hayes had ordered some whisky she cuttingly remarked, "I can drink clean and decent, and not with b——y lousy thieves."

At this she picked up her glass and threw some of her drink in John Rowley's face, then poured the rest into her mouth and spat it into Hannah's.

Charming.

Landlord Charles Jones complained about her conduct, and said Mrs Hayes had to leave. This sparked a heated argument, with Frederick Cotton asking whether she had called his wife 'lousy' and being struck by the woman for his trouble. All the parties left except Cotton and John Rowley, who no doubt looked at each other nonplussed. After finishing his drink John got up to leave, bidding his friend a good night. Thirty seconds later he came back, with a mouth full of blood.

Cotton asked, "Who did that?," and was told "That Hayes."

A man named William Elliott who had also been in the Black Swan happened to be leaving at the same time as John Rowley. James Hayes was waiting, and punched Rowley square in the face, saying "Here you b——d, take this; and now fetch your pals and I'll serve them the same."

After telling his friend what had happened, Cotton and Rowley went outside but found the street empty. Mr Cotton later told the magistrates what happened next:

> I was told by a woman not to take him home then. About a quarter to half an hour afterwards I took Rowley home. I found the court quiet, and there was no appearance of a row. About five minutes before I took Rowley home I saw a man standing at the entry leading to Rowley's court. I accompanied Rowley home because I felt he was in danger of Hayes and his wife. I remained with Rowley in his yard till the row began.

The 'row' was witnessed by watchmaker William Clare, who lived fruther along Spon Street at Chapel Yard and whose rear yard afford a clear view across a fence to 30 Court.

His evidence before the magistrates was of vital importance:

> When I got near the fencing I saw Mrs Rowley [Hannah Miller]. She was abusing Mrs Hayes. She went near to Mrs Hayes' door. I then saw Mars Hayes come out of her own house. She was turning up her sleeves. She said "Where is the b——d, with me or you." The two women met and commenced fighting. I then saw [James Hayes] come out of his house with a poker in his hand. I could not swear which end he had hold of. He said, "Where is the old b——d; I'll clear the b——y yard."
>
> He passed the women, who were fighting. Rowley was walking up the yard, and Hayes met him. I did not notice that Rowley had anything in his hand. I heard not more words pass. When they met I saw Hayes raise the poker and strike Rowley on the head. Deceased fell. I only saw Hayes strike him once. He fell instantaneously.

Joseph Adams, who had been in the Windmill Inn close to Court 30, heard the commotion and went to investigate. He helped Hannah's son from her first marriage, John Miller, carry John

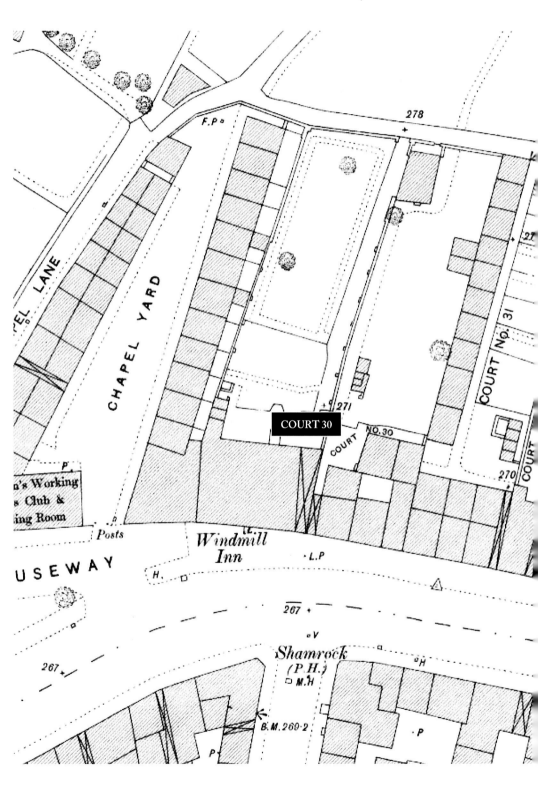

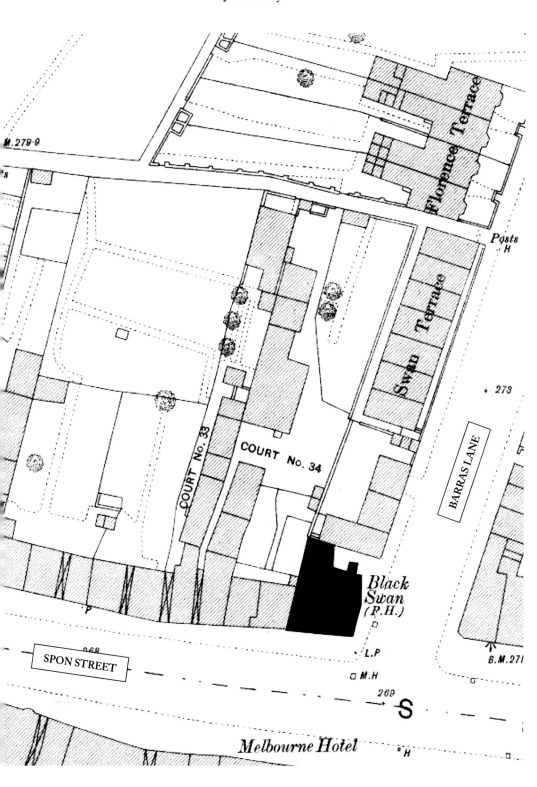

Rowley into the house.

Police Constable Blackshaw was called, arriving a few minutes past ten o'clock, and went into the Rowley's home. He was dead. The officer sent for a doctor and then apprehended James Hayes, who denied striking the dead man with a poker, saying it was his fist instead.

Dr John Overton, who was involved in the investigation into the death of baby Emma Golsby some thirty years earlier, happened to live on Spon Street so arrived just three or four minutes after being summoned. He noted marks around Rowley's head, including a radiating wound which indicated blood under the surface of the scalp, but the skull had not been fractured.

Crucially, after a post mortem the medical experts were of the opinion that death had been caused by John Rowley's head coming into contact with the ground as he fell, and *not* from the blow inflicted by Hayes with the poker.

At the magistrates' hearing at County Hall, on 28 September, James Hayes made the following statement:

> When I was at my house on the evening in question, there was a disturbance in the yard close to my door. I sent my lodger for my wife, and I was challenged to fight. I went out and saw my wife being ill-used. I was knocking a peg out of my boot with my poker, and I took it out accidentally, not thinking of using it. Rowley came up, and I gave him a blow with great force, and he fell. There was no bad blood existing between myself and Rowley, for he was a man I always liked. I struck him with my fist, and not with the poker.[231]

Before Mr Justice Denman at Warwick's Shire Hall, during the same Assizes at which Edward East (above) appeared, Hayes was charged with the wilful murder of John Rowley, but convicted of manslaughter when the jury agreed with the doctors that death had been caused by his head striking the flagstones rather than the blow itself.

231 *Coventry Standard*, 2 October 1874.

Hayes was sentenced to five years' penal servitude.[232]

*

Following his release James Hayes was reunited with the battling Elizabeth and the couple took their children to relocate on the other side of the city, at Castle Street.[233] Seemingly having learned his lesson, Hayes never appeared before the magistrates again.

Hannah, the common-law wife of John Rowley – now twice widowed – reverted to her first married surname of Miller and continued living at 2 House Court 30 for a good many years, earning her keep by taking in laundry.

She was still in the house at the time of the 1881 Census, seven years after the drunken argument at the Black Swan which resulted in tragedy, and eventually died in 1885.

232 *Coventry Herald*, 25 December 1874.
233 1881 Census.

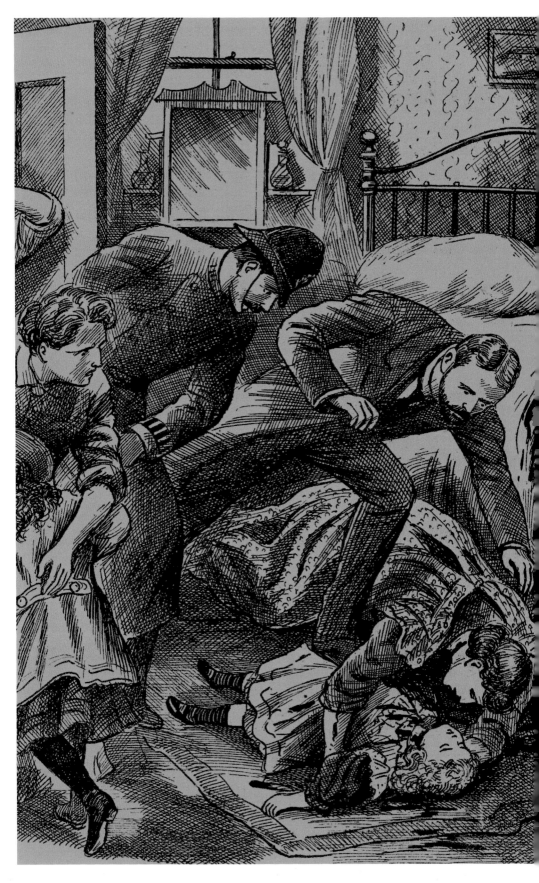